A History of The Westchester Cooperative and Its Neighbors

Peter T. Higgins

Copyright © 2024 by Peter T. Higgins
All rights reserved.
No portion of this book may be reproduced, by any process or technique, without the express written consent of the author.

All photographs used in this book were taken by the author unless otherwise noted. All photographs taken by the author remain the property of the author and may not be used without the express written consent of the author.

A History of
The Westchester Cooperative and Its Neighbors

An Historical Review

ISBN: 979-8-9874760-6-2

Tender Fire Books

www.TenderFireBooks.com

Author's Web site:
www.higgins-dc.com

Table of Contents

Introduction 1
Overview 5
Early History 7
    The 1700s 7
    The 1800s 10
    New Subdivisions Formed 13
        Fairview Heights Subdivision 14
        Tunlaw Heights Subdivision 15
    Some Facts From the End of the 19th Century 15
The First Half of the 1900s 16
    The Kennedy Brothers Purchase the Land and Plan Apartments 21
    The Westchester Development Corporation 1929-1937 22
    A Dutch Company Purchases the Westchester 1937 29
The 1940s and 1950s Bring Big Changes 33
    City Investing Purchases the Westchester 1947 33
    The Westchester Becomes a Cooperative 38
The Westchester Gets New Neighbors 43
    Development of 3900 Watson Place 43
    Development of the Colonnade 55
    Development of the Cathedral West 60
    Development of the Ginger Elkins Subdivision 68
In Conclusion 73
Appendix I: A Brief History of City Investing Company 75
Appendix II: Robert W. Dowling's Biography 77
Appendix III: The Copped Hall History 79
Acknowledgments 83

Table of Figures

Figure 1 DC Zoning Map - Squares 1805 and 1806 2

Figure 2 Winter Photograph of the Current Buildings – February 2007 3

Figure 3 Peace Cross 5

Figure 4 Peace Cross Inscription 6

Figure 5 Diagram of the Land Tracks by McNeil 9

Figure 6 1879 Map of the Second District of Washington, DC, Clipping 13

Figure 7 1892 U.S. Army Corps of Engineers Map, Clipping 14

Figure 8 1903 Baist's Map, Plate 18 Clipping 16

Figure 9 1911 Baist's Map, Plate 24 Clipping 18

Figure 10 Photograph of the Call Box Art 19

Figure 11 1922 Aerial Image of Our Neighborhood 20

Figure 12 The Westchester Sign on Cathedral Avenue 22

Figure 13 The Westchester's Main Building 25

Figure 14 View of the Sunken Garden Looking Toward Cathedral Avenue 26

Figure 15 View of the Sunken Garden Looking Toward The OB Building 27

Figure 16 1933 DC Highway Map, Clipping 28

Figure 17 1942 Letter to FDR Re: Ownership of the Westchester Apartments 29

Figure 18 The Copped Hall Gates at the Westchester 36

Figure 19 The Lion's Head Fountain at the Westchester 37

Figure 20 The Copped Hall Gates at Copped Hall 1910 38

Figure 21 Current DC Zoning Map, Clipping – the Westchester 41

Figure 22 Westchester A Building From the Hillside 42

Figure 23 Current DC Zoning Map, Clipping – 3900 Watson Place 45

Figure 24 The 3900 Watson Place B Building and Lawn 46

Figure 25 1960 Advertisement for 3900 Watson Place.. 47

Figure 26 View of the National Cathedral From the A Building... 48

Figure 27 1961 Advertisement of Watson Place Services 49

Figure 28 Perle Mesta Letter.. 54

Figure 29 Current DC Zoning Map, Clipping – the Colonnade 55

Figure 30 Colonnade Front Lawn and Trees... 57

Figure 31 Exterior Image of the Colonnade... 59

Figure 32 Current DC Zoning Map, Clipping – the Cathedral West 60

Figure 33 Bridge Leading to the Cathedral West 63

Figure 34 Side View of the Cathedral West Bridge 63

Figure 35 Cathedral West Fountains... 64

Figure 36 Cathedral West Swimming Pool Enclosure 66

Figure 37 Cathedral West Signage 67

Figure 38 Current DC Zoning Map, Clipping – Ginger Elkins Subdivision 68

Figure 39 The Seven Townhouses – Looking Southwest... 69

Figure 40 Rear View of the Townhouses 69

Figure 41 Townhouse Advertisement November 1968 70

Figure 42 Townhouse Advertisement December 1968.. 71

Figure 43 3921 Watson Place NW – From Coldwell Banker Advertisement................. 72

Figure 44 Copped Hall Photograph with Morning Fog... 82

For Kathy
June 4, 1948 - April 28, 2016

Introduction

When my wife, Kathy, and I moved into 3900 Watson Place in 2001, we already had lived in Washington since the early '70s. But independently, back in the '60s, each of us had stayed at 3900 Watson Place and eaten at the Westchester Dining Room.

In the '60s, my father, Joseph A. Higgins, worked for City Investing Corporation (City) in New York as Vice President for Real Estate and concurrently Vice President of the Realest Corporation (Realest), a City subsidiary. City operated the Westchester at one point in time and had already built 3900 Watson Place. Realest owned the land under the Westchester and 3900 Watson Place at some point – see the body of this book for details on these times. Kathy's grandmother, Gertrude Finn, also worked for City in the 1960s. In those days, City maintained an apartment at 3900 Watson Place and, as my father was on the Board of Directors of 3900 Watson Place representing both City and Realest, he would come down to DC and stay in that apartment.

Occasionally my mother and I would accompany my dad on those trips and we would all stay at the corporate apartment. When Kathy came to Washington to look at colleges, she and her parents also stayed in the apartment. About 50 years after my dad was on the 3900 Watson Place Board, I became president of that board and corporation. It was then that I discovered very early board meeting minutes and copied some facts from them; later, it appears those early minutes have been misplaced.

Fascinated by history, I decided to write the story of the land and buildings now occupied. It's a story that starts back in the 1700s and involves a lot of plans, not all of which came to fruition but which led to our beautiful buildings and campus. Initially, I had planned to focus on the 3900 Watson Place NW history, but the modern history of the land begins with the 1930 purchase of land by Gustave Ring's Westchester Development Corporation. Realizing this, I changed the focus of this book to the Westchester, 3900 Watson Place NW, the Colonnade, the Cathedral West, and the seven townhouses on Watson Place.

In 1947, City Investing purchased the Westchester and all of the land. In 1952 the president of City, Robert Dowling, purchased and installed the wonderful gates from Copped Hall that mark the entrance to the Westchester campus. I was fortunate enough to have a summer job for several years at the Carlyle Hotel in Manhattan, where Dowling lived. While working there, I had the opportunity to talk to him occasionally – he was, as they say, larger than life. To do Dowling justice, to explain City, and to provide some details on The Copped Hall Trust, I have added three appendices – one on City, one on Dowling's life, and one on Copped Hall.

The DC zoning map (Figure 1) shows the buildings and land that currently are on the 27.5 acres that Ring purchased in 1930 and then City purchased in 1947; the map spans from the Colonnade at the south to the Cathedral West at the north of the map. An aerial photograph of the same acreage, taken by the author, is Figure 2.

Figure 1 DC Zoning Map - Squares 1805 and 1806

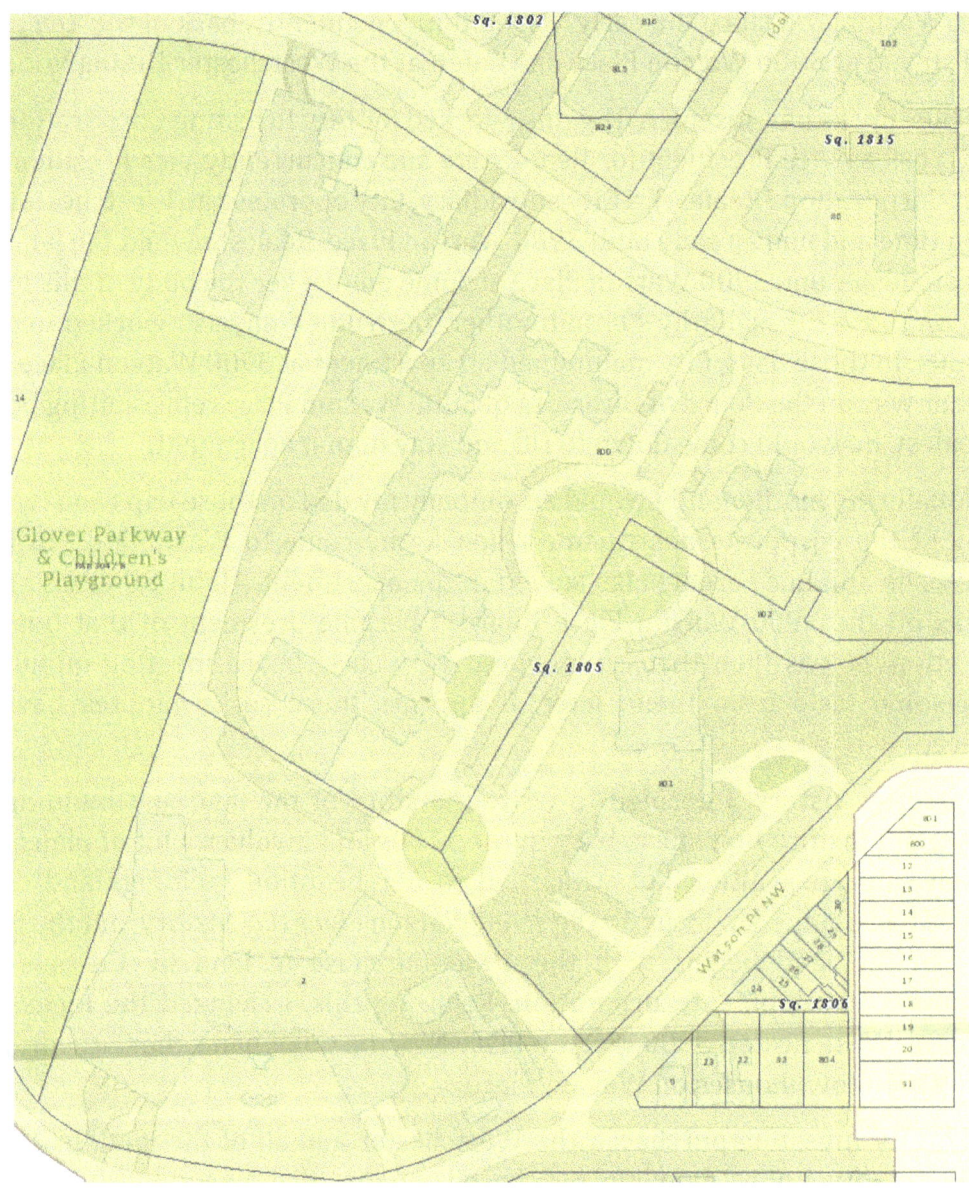

The following table is the code to the map in Figure 1.

Square	Lot	Community Name	Acreage
1805	1	Cathedral West	2.5
1805	2	The Colonnade	7.5
1805	800	The Westchester	10.46
1805	801 & 802	3900 Watson Place N.W. Inc.	5.5
1806	24 through 30	Townhouses – Ginger Elkins Subdivision	01.44

The last acre and a half, the townhouses, also includes the actual street – Watson Place.

Figure 2 Winter Photograph of the Current Buildings – February 2007

This winter photograph above shows the various communities from Cathedral West on the top left of the picture (south side of Cathedral Avenue) all the way to the Ginger Elkins townhouses on the right side of the picture (southeast side of Watson Place NW).

- The communities and their current street addresses:
    - Cathedral West (4100 Cathedral Ave.)
    - The Colonnade (2801 New Mexico Ave.)
    - The Westchester (3900-4000 Cathedral Ave.)
    - Ginger Elkins Townhouses (3909 - 3921 Watson Place)
    - 3900 Watson Place (3900 A & B Watson Place)

Please note that in searching the records of the District of Columbia there are references both to *Liber* and *Book* as well as to *folio* and *page*. They evolved over time from the Latin to the English names. For consistency, the Latin terms (Liber and folio) are used in this document.

In writing this book I have condensed abbreviations such as N. W., D. C. to NW, DC where practical. One clear exception is the formal name of 3900 Watson Place in the section on its development memorializing when the name was formally adopted March 1960 as: ***3900 WATSON PLACE N.W. INC.*** While the Certificate of Amendment of the Corporation used all capital and bold letters – the normal representation uses *title case* lettering: 3900 Watson Place N.W. Inc. The State of Delaware registered the name with a blank before the W of N.W. and thus the current legal corporate name is: 3900 Watson Place N. W. Inc.

Overview

The use of the land under our cooperatives, condominiums, and townhouses has changed substantially over the past 300 years. Looking at old maps and reading various histories of the area, we can trace the land ownership and use from the 1700 to today. The first changes, which still define our neighborhood, occurred in the last quarter of the 19th century, when subdivisions were established in the *highlands* of Washington.

Our neighborhood is dominated by views of the magnificent National Cathedral of Saints Peter and Paul, which was established in 1898. The establishment event is memorialized on the Peace Cross on the Cathedral Close – between the Bishop's House and St. Albans School; the picture below shows it in relation to the Cathedral.

Figure 3 Peace Cross

The cross bears an inscription memorializing the 1898 event as can be seen in Figure 4. Construction of the Cathedral started in 1907.

Figure 4 Peace Cross Inscription

The other most currently visible changes occurred starting in 1930, with the construction of many new buildings – the communities discussed in this book included – and the subdivision of the land into multiple properties.

Early History

This section traces the land ownership and use starting in the 1700s and going up to 1930, when Gustav Ring's Westchester Development Corporation assembled a block of 27.5 acres that today is home to the Westchester and its immediate neighbors.

The 1700s

The area now called Northwest Washington, DC, was then in Frederick County in the British Colony of Maryland. The name Maryland honors Queen Henrietta Maria (1609-1669), wife of Charles I (1600-1649), King of Great Britain and Ireland, who signed the 1632 charter establishing the Maryland colony.[1] According to the Frederick County website, *Frederick County was created in 1748 from Baltimore and Prince George's counties (Chapter 15, Acts of 1748). The County probably was named after Frederick Calvert (1731-1771), sixth and last Lord Baltimore, who was the Proprietor of Maryland from 1751 until his death in 1771 at Naples, Italy.*[2]

During the Revolutionary War the Constitutional Convention of 1776 (also known as the Second Continental Congress, which developed the Articles of Confederation[3]) separated a section of Frederick County and created Montgomery County. According to the Montgomery County website, *Montgomery County was formed by resolve of the Constitutional Convention of 1776 on September 6, 1776 (effective October 1, 1776). Created from Frederick County, Montgomery County was named for Revolutionary War hero General Richard Montgomery (1738-1775). Born in Swords, County Dublin, Ireland, General Montgomery died leading Continental forces against Quebec.*[4]

The United States Constitution was approved by the Constitutional Convention on Sept. 17, 1787, and ratified by the required ninth state, which happened to be New Hampshire, on June 21, 1788. The Constitution authorized the creation of a Federal District – referred to as *the seat of government* (US Constitution, Article I, Section 8, Clause 17). The Resident Act of 1790, as amended in 1791, established the guidelines

---

[1] http://msa.maryland.gov/msa/mdmanual/01glance/html/name.html
[2] http://msa.maryland.gov/msa/mdmanual/36loc/fr/html/fr.html
[3] Teaching American History.org at http://teachingamericanhistory.org/convention/intro/
[4] http://msa.maryland.gov/msa/mdmanual/36loc/mo/html/mo.html

for the location of the Federal District to be on the Potomac River, and it gave the president the authority to select the exact site. The relatively new Congress had elected George Washington president on Feb. 4, 1789. The original Federal District, *The Territory of Columbia*, had two counties (Washington and Alexandria counties as well as the City of Washington).[5] The area of interest, our 27.5 acres, was in Washington County. There are no longer counties in the District of Columbia.

Originally much of the property in this immediate area was part of three large tracts / patents (land grants):

- Alliance Farm
    - Carlton Fletcher reports in the Glover Park History website that John Threlkeld of Georgetown owned 812 acres in Washington County called Alliance.
    - In 1842 Agnes Levis acquired, from Clement Smith's estate about 156 acres of Alliance…[6]
- Lucky Discovery[7]
    - Granted to Thomas Pratt
    - Patent date: 11 July 1757
    - Size: 119 acres
- Scott's Ordinary (originally known as Scotch Ordinary)[8]
    - Granted to: Alexander Arthur
    - Patent date: 10 Sept 1716
    - Size: 100 acres

Fletcher provides a nice diagram, drawn by Priscilla W. McNeil in 1991, that shows the relationships of the three parcels of land listed above.[9]

---

[5] Carey & Lea Geographical, Statistical, and Historical Map of the District of Columbia, Philadelphia, 1822
[6] http://gloverparkhistory.com/estates-and-farms/alliance-farm/alliance-farm/
[7] Liber BC10 & BC11, as indexed in the Consolidated edition of Settlers of Maryland 1679-1783, Peter Wilson Coldham
[8] Liber FF7 & PL4, Maryland State Archives as indexed in Settlers of Maryland 1701-1730, Peter Wilson Coldham
[9] http://gloverparkhistory.com/geography/maps-places-features/maps/

A History of The Westchester Cooperative and Its Neighbors

Figure 5 Diagram of the Land Tracks by McNeil

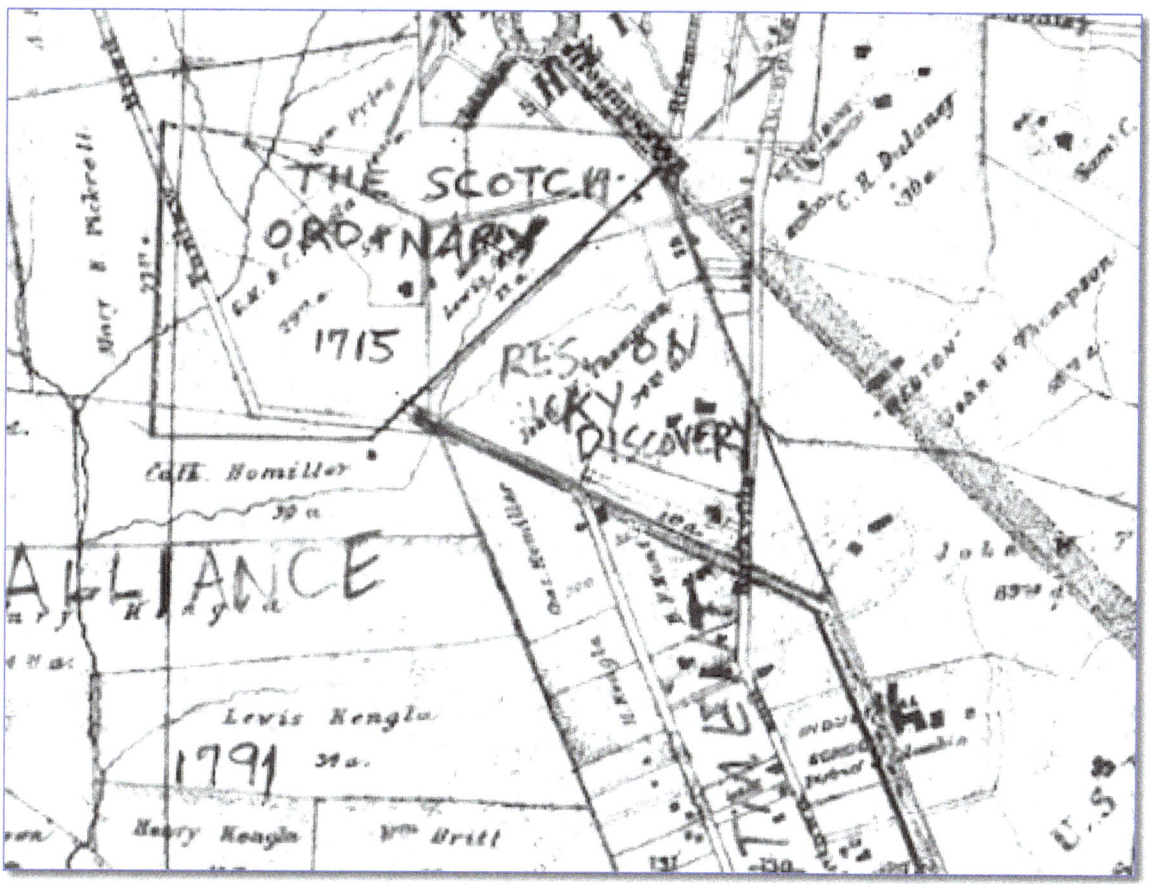

The land grants were made by the Maryland colonial powers not the king of England as is sometimes thought. The summary of the practice of land grants is explained both in the UK government archives and in the Maryland State Archives.

The UK records state:

> *In early colonial America, Britain considered land to belong to the Crown because it had been discovered and settled by its subjects.*
>
> *The Crown granted land to companies to organise settlements and sometimes to people as a reward for services.*
>
> *Although land grants were nominally made in the name of the Crown, most were made and recorded in the colonies rather than in London and these records may be available in American state archives.*[10]

While the Maryland records state:

---

[10] http://www.nationalarchives.gov.uk/help-with-your-research/research-guides/american-and-west-indian-colonies-before-1782/#10-land-grants

> *When King Charles I granted the Charter of Maryland to Cecil Calvert on June 20, 1632, he gave him ownership of all land within certain boundaries. Article XVIII of The Charter gave Lord Baltimore full authority to "assign, Alien, grante, demise, or enfeoff" any parcels [of the Province] to any persons willing to purchase the same. Down to the time of the Revolutionary War, all land grants in Maryland came from the Lords Baltimore, and after the death of Frederick, the 6th Lord Baltimore, from his son, Henry Harford, the Proprietor. It was the custom to date legal documents by the Regnal Year of the British Monarch, and this phraseology gave rise to the unfounded myth that Marylanders had "land grants from the King." Between 1634 and 1680, the Calverts encouraged settlers by promising to grant each settler so many acres (usually 50 acres) for himself and for each other person he or she brought into the Province. In 1680 this "head right" system was abolished, but Charles Calvert, 3rd Lord Baltimore, created the Land Office.*[11]

The 1800s

In March 1820 the Secretary of War wrote to Georgetown merchants Stull and Williams about the loan of 30 tons of gunpowder from the Ordinance Office for use in construction, etc. This was far too much gunpowder to store in Georgetown. According to Fletcher the City Council decided to seek land outside of Georgetown and ended up building a powder magazine on our land:

> *In 1821 John Threlkeld and Dr. Magruder were appointed by the City Council of Georgetown to purchase ground for a fireproof Powder Magazine. "The ground was bought from Elizabeth Nevitt in October, 1821, at the west end of a lane about 100 perches due west from Saint Alban's Church on the Rockville and Georgetown turnpike, and the house was built of brick, with a slate roof." (Handwritten note, Georgetown Ordinances, September 29, 1821)*

> *The road from High street extended, to the powder magazine, ran through the property of Mr. Wise, and through "Mr. Cammack's vegetable garden." This road–which appears to have been the precursor to Cathedral Avenue–ran west from what is now Wisconsin Avenue, then turned south into what is now the campus of the Westchester Apartments. ("The Road to the Powder House", Carbery's Book p.44, Office of the Surveyor; Georgetown Ordinances, March 3, 1829, September 23, 1835)*[12]

Our land can be traced to two large parcels from the early 1870s that were originally part of the land grants and Alliance Farm mentioned above. The two parcels were known as:

---

[11] http://guide.mdsa.net/pages/viewer.aspx?page=landrecords
[12] http://gloverparkhistory.com/institutions-cemeteries/institutions/former-institutions/the-georgetown-powder-magazine/

- The Jacob Kengla property (70 acres)
- The Agnes Levis property (60 acres)

In the Washington, District of Columbia City Directory, 1863, we see entries for:

- Henry Kengla butcher, Georgetown market, home – 401 High St.
- Jacob H. Kengla butcher, stalls 26 & 28 Georgetown market, home – Georgetown Heights.

In the 1870s Jacob H. Kengla owned about 70 acres west of (now) Wisconsin Avenue between Tunlaw (Walnut spelled backwards!) Road and (now) Massachusetts Avenue. His house was eventually razed to make way for Massachusetts Avenue.[13]

Agnes Levis died in 1873. Her estate assessed at 60 acres in 1876, had been divided into at least two parts. Philip Levis, born DC circa 1846, resided on the southern end of Alliance Farm, about where the Westchester is today.[14]

The ownership of these tracts of land in 1903 is shown on a Baist's map from that time (Figure 8). Some of the same names as in 1870 are still dominant in 1903. The change of fortune for the Levis family stems in part from an 1875 mortgage (explained below); by 1911 (Figure 9) the names had undergone only a few changes from 1903.

Philip Levis, in 1875, made a mortgage secured by a note to Charles R. Kengla and George M. Kengla. In 1878, upon Levis defaulting on the second trust, the trustee of the second mortgage sold the land to the Kenglas for $1,000 – far less than the real value. This case centered on *a bill in equity, filed by the mortgagor of land in the District of Columbia, more than fifteen years after the sale and conveyance of the land under a power in the mortgage, to redeem the land and to enforce a trust therein.* The U.S. Supreme Court decided on 21 February 1898 that the lower courts had decided correctly in dismissing the case.[15]

Directory searches for 1890 show Philip Levis as a butcher at the Northern Liberty Market - 5th and K St. NW. The market was gutted by a fire in 1946, and eventually torn down in 1985 after several incarnations including housing a wax museum from 1966 through 1974.[16]

The Kengla family comes up in the newspapers quite frequently in the 1860s and 1870s. Some of the news items from the *Evening Star* provide a view into the prices, culture, and activities of the times:

---

[13] http://gloverparkhistory.com/glover-park/residential-development-before-1926/cathedral-heights/
[14] http://gloverparkhistory.com/estates-and-farms/alliance-farm/alliance-farm/
[15] *Levis v. Kengla*, 169 U.S. 234, 1898
[16] http://ghostsofdc.org/2012/12/14/northern-liberty-market/

> 1868 – 19 August: Sale of Real Estate: Thomas Dowling, auctioneer, sold yesterday the property known as Jone's Soap Factory, on the upper road above Georgetown to Lewis Kengla, for $8,160.
>
> 1872 – 18 June: Chancery Sale of Valuable Real Estate near Georgetown: By virtue of a decree of the Supreme Court of the District of Columbia, sitting in equity, in a cause pending therein between Susan Kengla et al vs. Henry Green et al. we shall processed to sell, on the premises, on Thursday, the 20th day of June, A. 1872 at 6 o'clock p. m. all that piece or parcel of land ... being part of Scott's Ordinary ... containing about five acres of land, more or less, with the improvements. ... [and several other properties listed in the article].
>
> 1873 – 15 March: $5 REWARD. – Strayed from the premises of the undersigned, a black BUFFALO COW. The above reward will be paid for her return. J. P. Kengla, Linnaean Hill, Rock Creek.
>
> 1873 – 1 August: Land Sales: Jacob H. Kengla to E Brooker, 2.5 acres resurvey of "Lucky Discovery" on Rockville turnpike, $2,500.
>
> 1874 – 1 April: BY THOMAS DOWLING, AUCTIONEER, 641 LOUISIANA AVE., 2ND DOOR EAST OF 7TH STREET: TRUSTEE'S SALE OF IMPROVED PROPERTY ON TENNALLYTOWN ROAD, NEAR ST. ALBAN'S CHURCH. ... adjoins the former residence of the late Lewis Kengla.
>
> 1874 – 7 April: Thomas Dowling, auctioneer, sold yesterday, for W. D. Cassin, trustee, a two-story frame house, situated on the road to Tennallytown, to George Kengla & Bro., for $1,950.
>
> 1876 – 16 March: GEORGETOWN. CATTLE MARKET – [Reported by J. H. Kengla & Co] – Number of cattle on market, 213; number sold, 213; at prices ranging from 3.5 cts to (illegible) cts per pound. Number of cows and calves offered, 20; number sold, 20; at $20 - $45. There were no sheep on the market.
>
> 1877 – 30 January: GEORGETOWN. Relief. – Mr. Jacob Kengla has sent orders for 8 or 10 cords of wood to the St. Vincent's Society of Trinity (Catholic) church, which that association has distributed among the poor of Georgetown, doing much good.

To the best of my knowledge Thomas Dowling, auctioneer, is not related to Robert W. Dowling; the common last name appears to be an interesting coincidence.

In 1879 most of what is now the densely populated Wisconsin Avenue corridor was an extremely rural place as seen in the map below (Figure 6). Georgetown ran up into what is now the Glover Park commercial district. There were dirt roads between today's Wisconsin Avenue and Foxhall Road. The Foundry Brook and its tributaries were not confined to pipes as they are now in the Glover Archbold Park, and the St. Alban's Church was there but the adjacent land, now home to the National Cathedral, was the location of the home of Caroline Dulaney.

Figure 6 1879 Map of the Second District of Washington, DC, Clipping[17]

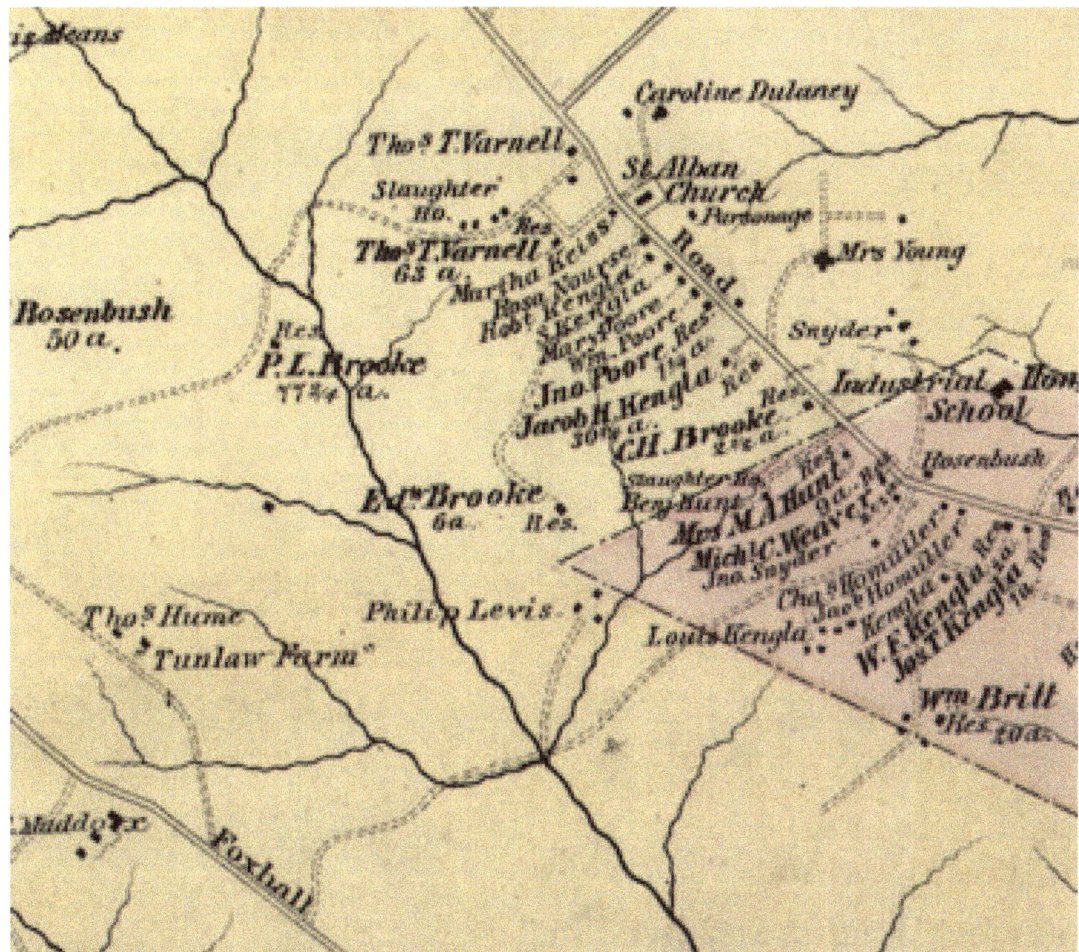

New Subdivisions Formed

The land in our neighborhood was divided into two subdivisions in 1890 that over time saw their names change. These subdivisions did not include our land but were indicators of significant changes to the area and the growth of the City of Washington. Originally the two subdivisions were:

- Fairview Heights
- Tunlaw Heights

They can be seen on the map from 1892 below along with Cleveland Heights, now Cleveland Park. Compare this to the 1903 map (Figure 8) – significant development was taking place with streets and lots allocated – the houses and buildings followed a little more slowly.

---

[17] http://ghostsofdc.org/

Figure 7 1892 U.S. Army Corps of Engineers Map, Clipping

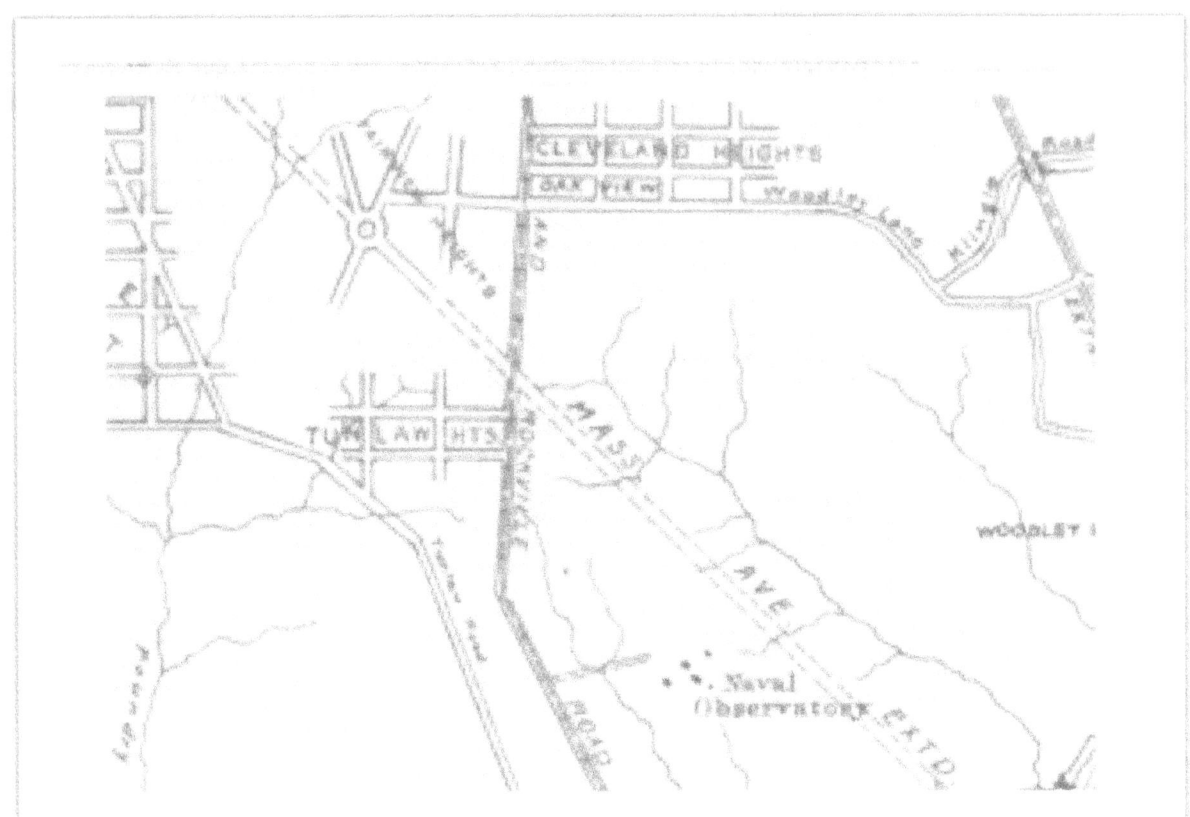

Fairview Heights Subdivision

By 1890 John Beall proposed the development of the Fairview Heights subdivision, north of our property, to take advantage of the proposed extension of Massachusetts Avenue, including the proposed Hamilton Circle where Idaho Avenue and 39th Street currently cross Massachusetts. One can still see the land preserved for this circle in the grassy areas that surround this intersection.

Hamilton Circle is still shown on many District maps and was the subject of a recent *Ghosts of DC* item: "Never Built Hamilton Circle at Massachusetts and Idaho."[18] The link takes you to a very short article and two excellent maps.

Beall's advertisement in *The Washington Post* on April 27 that year shows the prices for the land; they come out to be $10,890 per acre for the smaller lots and $8,712 per acre for the larger lots. But the lots were all much smaller than an acre.

---

[18] http://ghostsofdc.org/2016/07/08/hamilton-circle-massachusetts-idaho/

> *It is the intention of the syndicate owning this property to open streets, Massachusetts avenue and Hamilton circle, and to make some beautiful improvements, which will not be a tax upon purchasers of lots.*
>
> *We offer all unsold lots at twenty-five cents per square foot, and the first persons coming to secure them will get the best lots left at this figure. These lots will be sold on easy terms--1/4, 1/3, or ½ cash and balance to suit purchaser at 5 per cent interest. In connection with price, it is well to add that some lots at the rear having large areas will be sold at 20 cents per square foot. These prices are very low compared with those that will govern later, as from all the information now had upon the subject it is believed that in future sub-divisions of this section prices ranging from 50 to 75 cents per square foot will be asked and obtained.*[19]

Fairview Heights was to be just west of Georgetown and Rockville Road (now Wisconsin Avenue) – across from both a small subdivision called Cleveland Heights and where the National Cathedral now stands.

Tunlaw Heights Subdivision

In 1890 John W. Thompson subdivided 34 acres of former Kengla land north of Tunlaw Road and east of our property calling it Tunlaw Heights. At that point members of the Kengla family owned most of what is now our land.

There were four roads laid out in the Tunlaw Heights subdivision. According to the 1892 US Army Corps of Engineers map (Figure 7) they connected to Tunlaw Road and to the Georgetown and Rockville Road. What is now Cathedral Avenue was not even planned.

Some Facts From the End of the 19th Century

As recently as 1892:

- Massachusetts Avenue did not cross Rock Creek – the western extension had been proposed but not yet built (the current Massachusetts Avenue Bridge over Rock Creek was opened for use in 1941 – replacing a far smaller bridge).
- 39th Street was shown as ending on the southern end at Tunlaw Ave.
- Wisconsin Avenue was still called the Georgetown and Rockville Road.
- The National Cathedral was not yet planned.
- The 1892 U.S. Army Corps of Engineers map (Figure 7) already showed the proposed but never built Hamilton Circle where Massachusetts Avenue now crosses Idaho Avenue and 39th Street.

---

[19] http://gloverparkhistory.com/glover-park/residential-development-before-1926/cathedral-heights/

The First Half of the 1900s

At the beginning of the 20th century, the area around what is now the intersection of Massachusetts and Wisconsin avenues was the scene of planning, land speculation, and some development, but it was still farmland. The National Cathedral was still in the planning stages with construction starting on September 29, 1907, but St. Alban's Church was already there. Kengla family and Hemphill family members owned the 27.5 acres of land that is now apportioned to the Westchester and its neighbors.

Figure 8 1903 Baist's Map, Plate 18 Clipping

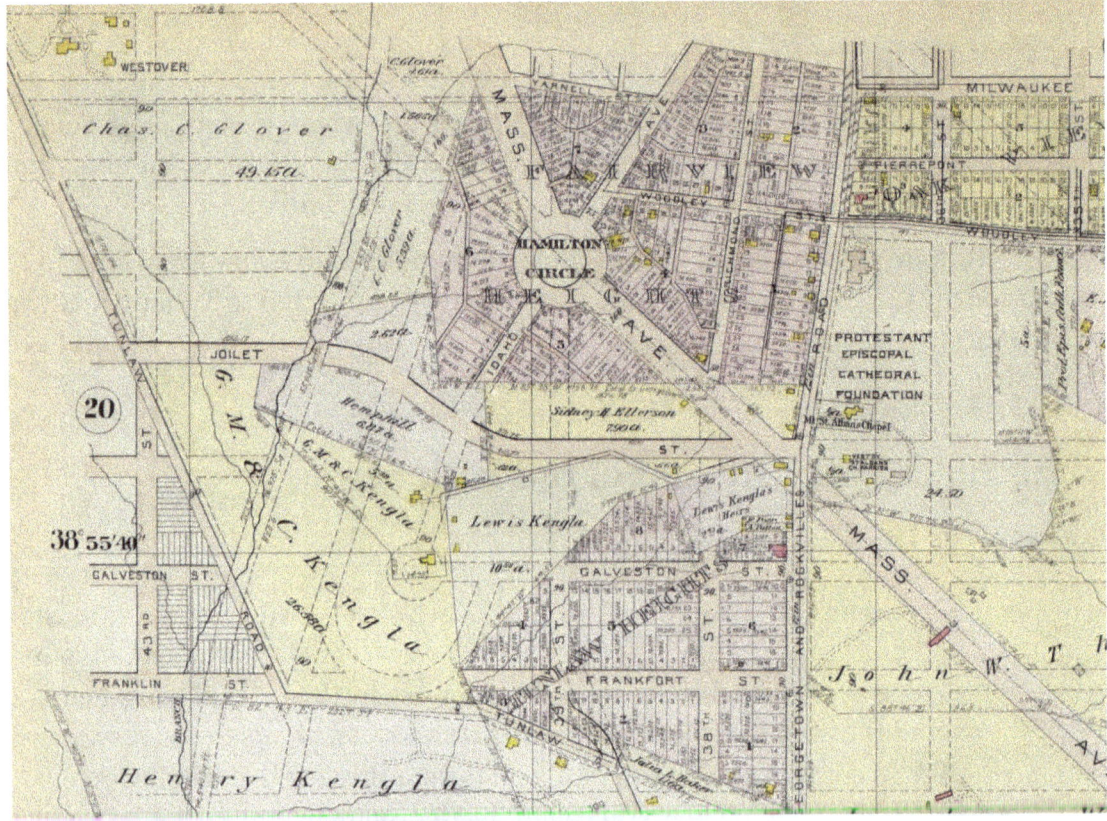

Looking at the 1903 Baist's map, above, we can see that the land where our campus is today was basically undeveloped. There was a house or two on it but most of the streets in the neighborhood were not yet completed. Watson Place itself was still just a concept without a name. Some interesting things stand out:

- Garfield Avenue (then known as Galveston Street) and 39th Street both ended where they met.
- Fulton Street (then known as Frankfort Street) went about a block farther west of 39th Street and dead-ended.
- 39th St. appears to connect to Tunlaw Road at the south end, while at the north end 39th Street was proposed to go only as far as Massachusetts Avenue, where the Hamilton Circle remained on the map as shown in 1892.
- Massachusetts Avenue appears to be shown coming out of Hamilton Circle to the northwest where 39th Street is now.
- Cathedral Avenue was Joliet Street (misspelled on the map as Joilet) and Idaho Avenue was proposed but not yet built south of Massachusetts.
- Watson Place is shown as a proposed street that was to be a semi-circular affair but is unnamed – see the 1911 Baist's map (Figure 9) for the later use of the name Watson Place NW.

In 1907 Tunlaw Heights was renamed Cathedral Heights, according to some sources,[20] but the 1911 map identifies the old Tunlaw Heights as Cathedral Highlands not Cathedral Heights. That spring Massachusetts was extended all the way to Wisconsin Avenue.[21]

On Sept. 29, 1907, the National Cathedral construction started with the foundation stone being laid. The National Cathedral website reports: *President Theodore Roosevelt and the Bishop of London spoke to a crowd of 10,000. The stone itself came from a field near Bethlehem and was set into a larger piece of American granite. On it was the inscription: "The Word was made flesh, and dwelt among us" (John 1:14).*[22]

In 1911 our land was still mostly undeveloped. Again, on the 1911 map (from the Baist's Real Estate Atlas of the District of Columbia), we note some interesting things:

- Galveston Street had been renamed to Garfield Street.
- Frankfurt Street had been renamed to Fulton Street.
- Joliet Street had been renamed to Jewett Street (now Cathedral Avenue).
- Charles C. Glover now owned a portion of the east side of the land where our campus is located, while George M. and Charles R. Kengla still owned the western side and the Hemphill family still owned a small northern portion.
- Idaho was proposed but not yet constructed south of Massachusetts.

---

[20] http://gloverparkhistory.com/glover-park/residential-development-before-1926/cathedral-heights/
[21] http://ghostsofdc.org/2012/04/27/move-to-cathedral-highlands-an-unobstructed-view-of-the-entire-surrounding-country/
[22] https://cathedral.org/history/timeline/

- Watson Place is shown as the name of the proposed street that was still planned to be a semi-circular affair.

Figure 9 1911 Baist's Map, Plate 24 Clipping

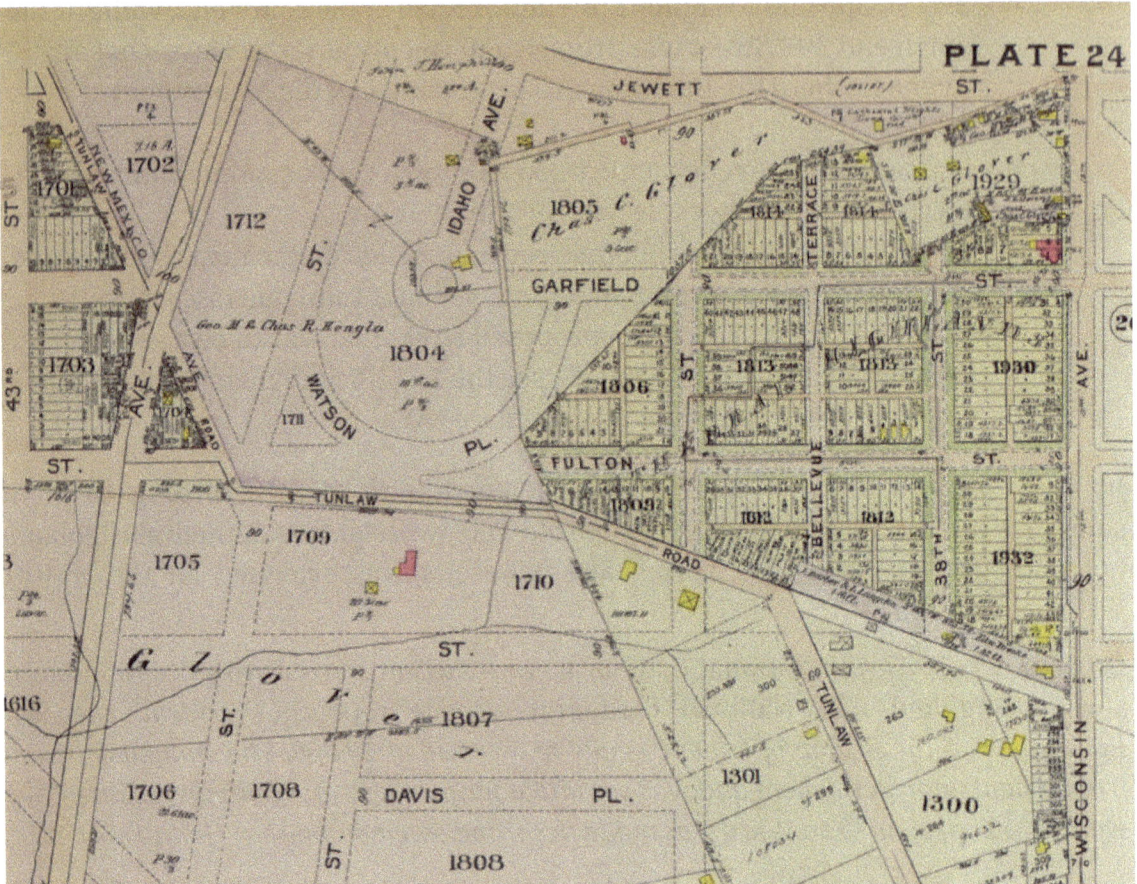

Until the 1920s some stories state that there were more cows than people in Cathedral Heights. There is an old police call box at the corner of Fulton Street and Bellevue Terrace that provides a brief history of the Kengla Farms and has a fanciful painting of what the neighborhood looked like – see the artist's rendition (Figure 10). Interestingly the artist chose to have all the cows facing the same way – perhaps it was dinnertime and they were headed home.

The other side of the call box identifies the artist as Peter Waddell and provides some information on the source of funding for the project as well as a history of the Kengla Farms:

> *Until the 1920s, Cathedral Heights was richer in cows than people. The neighborhood was carved into plots of woodland and farms, including nearly 30 acres owned by Henry Kengla on which the Westchester Cooperative Apartments now stand. The Kengla family had lived in the Washington area since the late 1700s. They were master butchers of German extraction with a stand at the*

Central Market on what is now the site of the National Archives. The Kengla brothers bought cows and sheep at Drover's Market near the Georgetown Reservoir and drove the stock along the dusty Cathedral Avenue to graze on their farms until slaughter. As business increased with the population of the city, Henry Kengla steadily accumulated land. At his death on 1903, he left an estate worth more than $200,000.

Figure 10 Photograph of the Call Box Art

Figure 11, an aerial photographic mosaic map of Washington, DC, 13 September 1922[23], shows exactly how rural our land was less than 100 years ago. This clipping

---

[23] https://www.loc.gov/resource/g3851a.ct004537/

from a much larger map shows Massachusetts running left to right. Above Massachusetts one can see the track for St. Alban's School as well as the early construction of the National Cathedral. South of Massachusetts, on the west side of Wisconsin, the old Mt. Alto Veterans Hospital can be seen. Our land can be seen in the center of the lower half of the picture as mostly cleared land, in a sort of circular pattern. The newly planted trees along the new streets in the various developments are clearly seen, as well, on the right hand side of the picture.

Figure 11 1922 Aerial Image of Our Neighborhood

Interestingly there was a building in Washington called the Westchester Apartment built in 1912. It has no relation to Ring's 1930 Westchester Apartments other than the extreme similarity of the names. There were several interesting news stories about the other Westchester in the 1914 - 1920 period. Two highlights are presented here:

- Aug. 29, 1914 Evening Star: A *deed has been placed on record transferring the ownership of the Westchester Apartment, on O street between 15th and 16th streets northwest, from Bates Warren to H. Latane Lewis. The Westchester is a four-story building containing sixteen apartments. It was erected about two years ago.*
- June 19, 1920 The Washington Herald: Headline: *GRANT 100 PCT. RENT PROFIT: The Rent-Commission yesterday allowed G. T. Howard, of the Westchester Apartment, 1333 Fifteenth street northwest to sublet his apartment at a rent of $100 a month, furnished. Howard rented the apartment from L. S. Fristoe for $50 a month, unfurnished. Fristoe entered no objections to Howard subletting the apartment.*

The Kennedy Brothers Purchase the Land and Plan Apartments

In 1921 the Kennedy Brothers Company (Edgar Sumter Kennedy and William Munsey Kennedy) bought a large piece of the eventual Westchester campus with the intent to build an apartment house.[24] In searching the records for the aforementioned sale one finds a couple of deeds registered with the District but not the 1921 deed. The company had started building homes and apartment buildings in the District of Columbia back in 1909. The Kennedy Brothers Company collaborated with Monroe Warren to build the Kennedy-Warren Apartment Building on Connecticut Avenue – just north of the National Zoo.

A significant sale was recorded in the District records on 14 July 1925 and is currently indexed to microfilm roll 5543 and frame 450. The sale was made by Elizabeth H. Hemphill, widow and sole devisee of John J. Hemphill, who sold William Kennedy a portion of the land she had inherited from her husband. The deed states that *the land is adjacent to the part of said tract conveyed to William M. Kennedy by deed dated Nov. 24, 1923.*[25] These records are incomplete in the District's online service, providing just two pages of a larger document. The online service does not reflect the sale of any other lands to Kennedy.

William Kennedy was living at 3900 Cathedral Ave. when he died on June 17, 1927, after having been in ill health for several years. Prior to Kennedy living there, Wilson M. Compton had lived there in 1925. Before that, it had been the Kengla home.[26] The house at 3900 Cathedral Ave. was about 100 years old at this point and was known as the Kennedy House after William moved there. On the 1911 map, it's shown as being on a circle where Idaho Avenue and Garfield Street were to intersect – something that never happened.

---

[24] Goode, James M., *Best Addresses*, page 300
[25] DC Deeds, Roll 5543, Frame 450
[26] "Landmark Replaced: Westchester Apartments on Site of Historic Home," *Washington Times*, Jan. 5, 1935

While the Kennedy Brothers were accumulating land, in 1924 Charles Carroll Glover and Anne Mills Archbold donated the land, known today as Glover Archbold Park, to the federal government. A portion of the parkland is directly adjacent to the west of our property. At some point there were plans for a children's playground in Glover Archbold Park between New Mexico and Massachusetts avenues. The playground, although never built, is still shown on DC government zoning maps. The park permits one to walk south to the Potomac River as well as north to Wisconsin Avenue and Upton Street – all in beautiful woodlands. Foundry Branch streambed runs through the park to the Potomac, most of the water on the surface is run off – the old stream is buried in a pipe.[27] John Bray notes on his website that *The narrow Park runs past Foxhall Village and Georgetown University, stretching nearly 3 miles from the C&O Canal to Van Ness Street, a length where "Silent Spring" author Rachel Carson once led birding hikes.*[28]

The Kennedy House must have been quite large as in 1928 it was leased to the La Colline School, a boarding school for boys and girls between the ages of 4 and 14, which was run by Mrs. Albert J. Myer, who was known as Baroness Irene Ungern. Many documents state that it was a finishing school for girls, but the school placed routine announcements in the newspaper about the opening of Fall 1928 classes and each states that La Colline is *"a boarding school for boys and girls between the ages of 4 and 14."*[29] By 1934 the Kennedy House had been torn down and Baroness Ungern was running the Academy of Languages at 1737 Connecticut Ave. The Academy taught French, German, Italian, Russian, and Spanish. The fee was $4 per month.[30]

The Westchester Development Corporation 1929-1937

Figure 12 The Westchester Sign on Cathedral Avenue

According to James M. Goode's *Best Addresses*, the plan for the Westchester was conceived in 1929 by Washington developer Gustave Ring.[31] According to US Census

---

[27] https://thehoe.org/2016/09/09/runoff-glover-archbold-national-park/
[28] https://thehoe.org/2016/08/19/thffthduhth/
[29] *Evening Star*, Sept. 9, 1928, page 102
[30] *Evening Star*, Sept. 30, 1934, page 32
[31] Goode, James M., *Best Addresses*, page 300

records, Ring was born in West Virginia on 17 January 1904[32] and by 1930 he was married and living in DC, where he was listed as *a manager in the Building Industry.*[33]

In 1930, the Kennedy property and other lands were purchased by the Westchester Development Corp. Some of the highlights of the purchases are to be found in the deeds registered with the District, as listed below:

January 30, 1930: George F. Hunt sold three parcels to the Westchester Development Corporation; the deed was registered with the District on 8 March 1930 on Microfilm roll 6418, frame 077:

- Parcel 1 running from the corner of the land dedicated for the Glover Parkway and Cathedral Avenue running 2,135 feet along Cathedral then south 1,307 feet to Tunlaw Road Along Tunlaw 332 feet to the edge of Glover Parkway. Then 627 feet along the eastern edge of the parkway back to Cathedral.
- Parcel 2, which appears to be directly east of parcel 1, starting at Tunlaw Road. and the southwest corner of Lot seven in Square 1809 running west along Tunlaw 578 feet to a gas pipe and then north to the southerly line of Cathedral Avenue then easterly 303 ft. to the edge of the proposed 39th Street. From there along the west side of the proposed 39th Street back to the start - a distance of 1,316 ft. *Excepting a parcel 40 feet by 40 feet conveyed to the Corporation of Georgetown For a powder magazine.*
- Parcel 3, a smaller parcel which starts at the same point on Tunlaw Road as Parcel 2 and runs 34 ft. north along the northerly line of Tunlaw 69 ft. to a stone, then north 145 ft. and south 204 ft. to the starting point.

8 March 1930: A Trust was recorded with the District, on Microfilm roll 6426, frame 051, to document a loan of $100,000 by The Westchester Development corporation by John H. Holmead. The trustees were Luther Swartzell and Edmund Rheem. The loan was a partial payment, in addition to the $660,000 first deed of trust, for the following parcel, which appears to be a subset of Parcel 3 (directly above) as it also includes the Georgetown powder magazine:

- Parcel 31 lot 80: Beginning at the southwest corner of the intersection of Cathedral Avenue and the proposed 39th St. South along the west line of 39th St. for 287 ft. then west 144 ft., north 260 ft., north 231 to the south line of Cathedral then along that line for 257 ft. back to the start.

---

[32] New York State, Passenger and Crew Lists, 1917-1966, arrival record for a 1958 Pan Am flight from Paris, accessed via Ancestry.com

[33] 1930 United States Federal Census, Washington, DC, Enumeration District No. 394, sheet 27A, accessed via Ancestry.com

> *Excepting a parcel 40 feet by 40 feet conveyed to the Corporation of Georgetown for a powder magazine.*

26 March 1930: D. Morton Levy sold a parcel north of Cathedral Avenue to the Westchester Development Corporation; the deed was recorded with the District, on Microfilm roll 6431, frame 132:

- Parcel 1: Beginning at the north line of Cathedral Ave. and the center line of the proposed 39th St. West along the north line of line of Cathedral Ave. for 349 ft. then north 189 ft. then 89° east 346 ft. to the center line of proposed 39th St. then south along that line for 251 ft. back to the start.

The Westchester Development Corp. planned to build "the largest apartment south of New York City."[34] The other developers were Morris Cafritz and Harvey Warwick, the architect of the Westchester.[35] According to Goode, Cafritz and Warwick were junior partners in the Westchester Development Corporation.

The vision was a $10 million construction project with eight buildings and almost 1,000 units. The architecture was somewhat mixed but has been described as *Moorish Revival*. Construction started in March 1930. The first buildings constructed were the ones on Cathedral Avenue – the OB short for the *Original Building* or the *Old Building* (both of these later names are used) and the A Building.

The District issued a building permit for the OB, Central, and Main construction on 5 March 1930 – Permit #13047. That April 10th the permit for Westchester A was issued – Permit #131963. These permits can be found in the DC Historical Building Permits Database – indexed online and available on Microfilm.[36]

The current Westchester website mentions the five buildings that exist today. They are the A Building, The OB, the Center Building, and the Main Building with two wings – the East and West buildings. While *Best Properties* and other reference material document four buildings (A, OB, Center, and Main), the Westchester rightly defines its own buildings on its website: three separate buildings in the one physical building – they are the East and West portions of the Main Building and the Center Building. This is similar to airports where, for instance, Terminals B and C are in the same physical building but are considered separate terminals.

When the Great Depression caused funding to dry up, only four of the eight planned buildings had been constructed – for a total of 556 units, ranging from efficiencies to three-bedroom suites. The Westchester Development Corporation had spent $4 million at that point. The event that brought a halt to construction was the voluntary bankruptcy of the mortgage-banking house, Swartzell, Rheem & Henesy. The Justice

---

[34] "Landmark Replaced: Westchester Apartments on Site of Historic Home," *Evening Star*, Jan. 5, 1935
[35] *Evening Star*, April 1, 1950, page B-1
[36] https://dcgis.maps.arcgis.com/apps/webappviewer/

Department's Bureau of Investigation (a forerunner of today's FBI) was reported as investigating the possible violation of banking laws. A January 1931 newspaper story reports that besides the legal issues, two major construction projects were halted pending results of the voluntary bankruptcy: the Westchester and the New Shoreham Hotel.[37]

Figure 13 The Westchester's Main Building

The largest of the planned buildings, the principal building with a pool and other amenities, was to be situated where the Colonnade Condominium building is now located. Prior to the construction of the Colonnade the land was flat and then dropped off to Tunlaw Road and New Mexico Avenue.

The Westchester apartment buildings opened in October 1931 as rental units and had 40 hotel rooms for guests of residents. Rooms for guests are still offered to residents some 80 years later. The Main Building, with its large porte-cochère, is shown in the recent image (Figure 13) taken from Building A of the 3900 Watson Place Cooperative.

The Westchester has indoor parking for a total of 300 spots. There was a Dining Room (open from 7:30 in the morning to 8:30 in the evening) that would deliver meals to apartments, a drug store, a Piggly Wiggly market, a beauty salon, and a barbershop.[38]

---
[37] *Evening Star*, Jan. 28, 1931, page A-2
[38] http://ghostsofdc.org/2012/06/20/the-westchester/

One of the prides of the Westchester is its large, elliptical, sunken garden with a wonderful fountain. The fountain was rebuilt in 2016 and is turned on seasonally. The recent pictures (Figures 15 & 16) show the fountain and surrounding garden. The land under the garden is owned partially by the Westchester and partially by 3900 Watson Place.

Figure 14 View of the Sunken Garden Looking Toward Cathedral Avenue

By the time construction stopped in 1931, the land where the rest of the Westchester apartment buildings were to have been built had been partially cleared. There is an excellent aerial photograph of the property on page 301 of *Best Addresses*. That photograph, taken in 1933, shows the completed buildings, the sunken garden and the two cedar alleys as well as the cleared land and the flat, grassy land where the principal building was to be located. That photograph was taken almost 20 years before the Victorian Gates were installed, as documented later in this book.

Figure 15 View of the Sunken Garden Looking Toward The OB Building

In August 1931 the Westchester Development Corporation deeded access to land for the construction of a sewer line along the route of the *current* Watson Place. Note, in the 1933 map (Figure 16) that Watson Place was now shown with roughly the same alignment as it was eventually constructed and paved in the 1960 time frame. Only the connection to Garfield Street is slightly more reasonable as built. The land is described in the deed:[39]

> A strip of land ten (10) feet wide, through a tract of land in the District of Columbia, recorded in the Office of the Surveyor, D.C., as Parcel 31/87, the center line of said strip of land being described as follows: Beginning on the north building line of Fulton Street at a point two (2) feet south of the center line of proposed Watson Place, and running thence in a northeasterly direction parallel to and two (2) feet south of the center line of said proposed Watson Place for, a distance of six hundred fifty (650) linear feet, more or less, to a point two (~) feet south of the center line of Garfield Street, extended; thence in an easterly direction parallel to and two (2) feet south of said center line of Garfield Street, extended, for a distance of sixty (60) linear feet, more or less, to the west side of

---

[39] The deed was stamped as being recorded by the DC government on 31 March 1932 with a number of 7830. But there is an annotation that it was "Delivered to the District of Columbia on 2 August 1932."

39th Street, as shown on the plat hereto attached as a part hereof and therein construct a sewer, as the Commissioners of the District of Columbia may direct, ...

In 1933 the DC government planned two roads for the then Westchester property. The Watson Place extension of Garfield Street and 42nd Street, which was to run from where the Colonnade Condominium is now located north along the Glover Archbold Park to Massachusetts Avenue, passing through the current location of the Cathedral West Condominium. In addition government plans included running Arizona Avenue right up the middle of Glover Archbold Park.[40]

The map on Figure 16, below is a snippet from the DC Government Highway Map of 1933.[41] It has playgrounds and recreation areas indicated by red outlines. Our 27.5 acres are where the word PLAYGROUND appears. This map shows 39th Street connecting to Tunlaw Road – as well as the Hamilton Circle. The red box around the abbreviation AVE. reflects a proposed playground as well as the proposed Arizona Avenue.

Figure 16 1933 DC Highway Map, Clipping

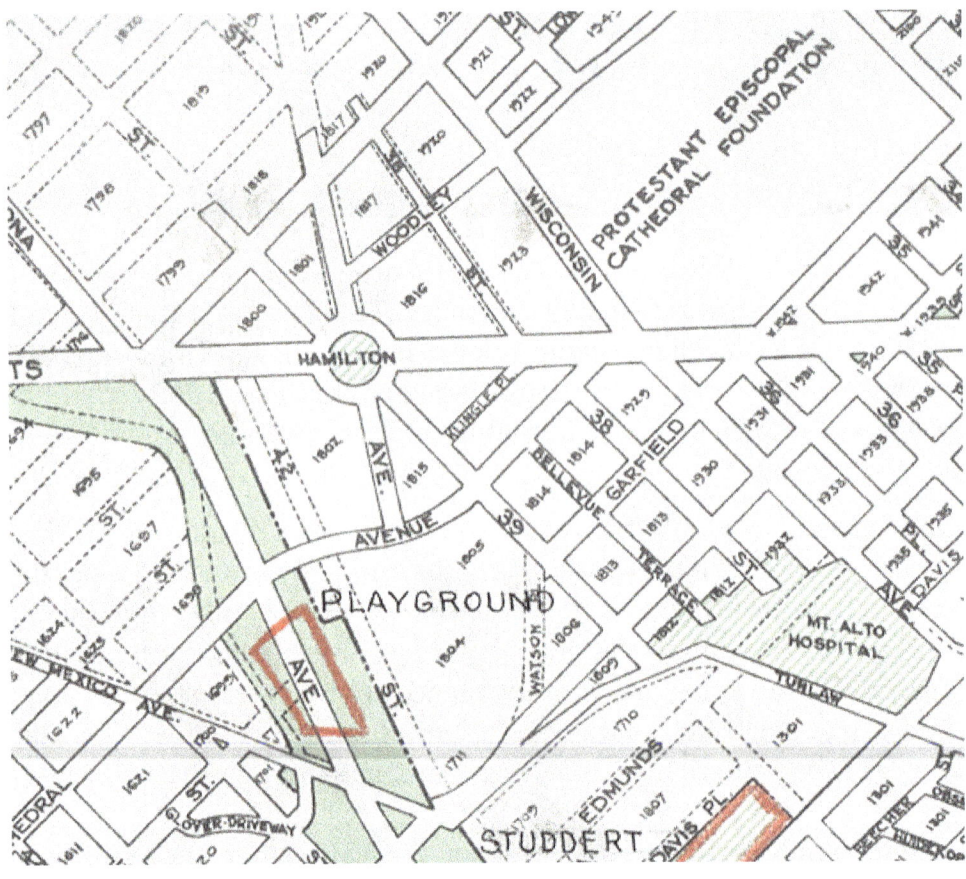

---

[40] Arizona Avenue and 42nd Street were previously shown on the 1911 Baist's map.
[41] Map of permanent system of highways, District of Columbia: Northwest quadrant; Office of the Surveyor; Office of the Engineer Commissioner DC; 1933

A Dutch Company Purchases the Westchester 1937

In 1937, needing to focus on other projects, Gustave Ring's Westchester Development Corporation sold the Westchester to an investment company, Amsinck, Sonne, & Company's arm, The Westchester Apartments, Inc. A Dutch bank, Nederlandische Standart Bank, in turn had funded this investment company.

An interesting part of this Dutch bank and the Westchester relationship is to be found in a 5 January 1942 memorandum from Treasury Secretary H. Morgenthau, Jr. to President Franklin Delano Roosevelt. There was a cover note and a three-page report.[42] The cover note is shown in Figure 17 and then a summary of the report follows.

Figure 17 1942 Letter to FDR Re: Ownership of the Westchester Apartments

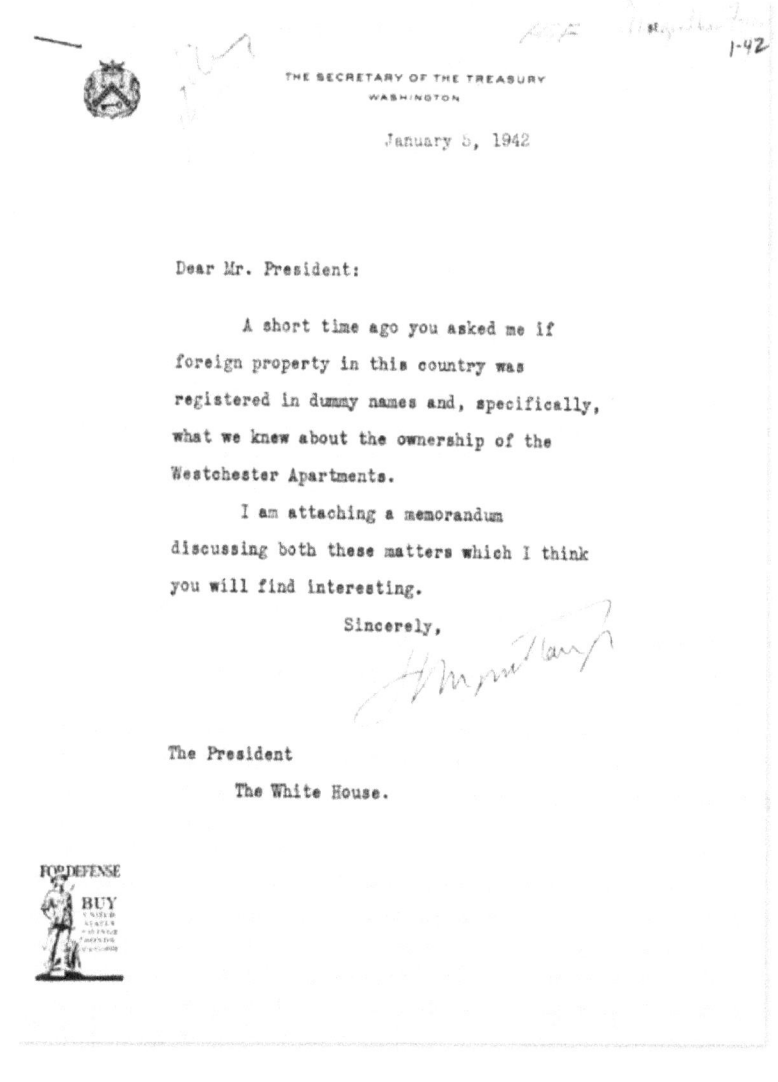

[42] http://www.fdrlibrary.marist.edu/_resources/images/psf/psfb000289.pdf

Here are the pertinent portions of Morgenthau's report:

> *As a first step in ferreting out the large amount of foreign owned properties held in the United States, the Treasury Department months ago required detailed reports to be filed with respect to all such properties. How these reports are being used is illustrated by the case to which you referred, that of the Westchester Apartments.*
>
> *From the property census report filed by the Westchester Apartments, Inc. and from supplementary reports of Treasury investigators, we have been able to construct the following picture:*
>
> *During 1938 and 1939 a Netherlands bank, the Nederlandische Standart Bank, transferred over $5,000,000 to the United States. This Netherlands bank was formed primarily to handle the investments of a family named Ofenheim. The four known members of this family are said to reside in various parts of the British Empire. The funds of other persons in the Netherlands were, however, accepted for investment by the Nederlandische Standart Bank. The funds transferred to the United States were placed unconditionally under the control of Hans Christian Sonne, an American of Danish extraction who has a substantial interest in two New York corporations, Amsinck, Sonne & Company, and Amsinck Sonne Corporation. Sonne formed the Neal Bancroft Corporation, a management corporation to handle the funds thus entrusted to him. This name has no significance but was compounded by selecting two names at random from the New York telephone directory. The assets of this corporation consist of various properties purchased with the $5,000,000. Sonne has stated that a complete list of the owners of the funds transferred by the Nederlandische Standart Bank was never revealed to him or any one else in the United States, One of the investments of the Neal Bancroft Corporation consists of a substantial portion of the outstanding stock of the Westchester Apartments, Inc. Most of these shares are held by Amsinck, Sonne & Company for Neal Bancroft Corporation. Hans Christian Sonne filed a TFR-300 report setting forth that he held the majority interest in the Westchester Apartments, Inc. as nominee for interests "believed to be British". However, from our investigation it is clear that both the Neal Bancroft Corporation and Westchester Apartments, Inc. are nationals of a blocked country, the Netherlands. Mr. Paul F. Myers, attorney for the Westchester Apartments, Inc. has stated to a Treasury representative that he is completely convinced that Queen Wilhelmina has no interest in the apartments. While this matter is still under investigation it is now established that Netherlands funds were being concealed by the "trust device" and the "holding company device".*

No further mention can be found of the investigation. (A FOIA Request submitted by the author to the Treasury Department in January 2017 showed that the Treasury Department had turned all TFR-300 and related records over to the National Archives and that the transfer logs did not show any material relevant to the Westchester investigation.) But we know that the ownership remained with the Westchester Apartments, Inc. and its Dutch masters, as in 1947 they sold the property – some stories point to needing the money back in Holland for restoration necessitated by war damage.

According to the New York Secretary of State's files, Amsinck, Sonne, & Company was registered on 1 February 1938 in New York City.[43] In an obituary of Hans C. Sonne we read that *he served as chairman of Amsinck, Sonne & Co., a merchant-banking concern, from 1923 to 1955.*[44] Thus throwing some confusion on the actual start date of this company in the U.S. and possibly confused the investigators.

The sale was completed on June 1, 1937, and reported in the *Evening Star* the next day. The sale price was in excess of $4 million. Morris Cafritz, Gustave Ring, and Harvey Warwick held the Westchester Development Corporation stock that was sold to an international business syndicate, represented by Amsinck, Sonne, & Co. The new owners planned to erect additional apartments on the undeveloped land.[45]

Ring's other activities in the late 1930s included the development, construction, and operation of the 1,000-unit housing development Colonial Village in Arlington, Va.[46] The project was an experiment in low-cost housing. The rent was to be $10 per room per month. Construction started in January 1939 and the buildings were to be ready for occupancy that July. The project was the result of two years of planning and analysis by Ring with cooperation from the Washington office of the Federal Housing Authority.[47]

In 1940 Ring was named *as consultant for Defense Housing Coordinator C. F. Palmer for the National Defense Commission.*[48] Early in 1942, Ring entered the army as a major.[49] He served until August 1944.[50] After the war, Ring went on to construct more buildings. In March 1950 his Ring Construction Company of Washington, DC, purchased a vacant lot in Pittsburg for a half-million dollars, planning a 20-story apartment building that was to include shops, a garage, and 570 apartment units.[51]

Professional observations on the Architecture of the Westchester:

The Westchester architecture of the early 1930s has been recognized by the Society of Architectural Historians in their book Buildings of the District of Columbia, published September 9th, 1993 by the Oxford University press. The Westchester was covered in the section entitled Rock Creek Park and Northwest Washington. The following is a candid analysis 63 years after the design was memorialized in blue

---

[43] Entity Source website – NY Secretary of State file number 50649
[44] *New York Times*, Aug. 4, 1971, page 37
[45] *Evening Star*, June 2, 1937, front page
[46] *Evening Star*, March 20, 1939, page A-13
[47] *Evening Star*, Jan. 14, 1939, page B-1
[48] *Evening Star*, Aug. 30, 1940, page B-4
[49] *Evening Star*, May 23, 1942, page B-4
[50] US Department of Veterans Affairs BIRLS Death File, 185-2010, accessed via Ancestry.com
[51] *Evening Star*, March 30, 1950, page A-2

prints and buildings. Many of us would disagree with their final assessment but it does provide a professional's vocabulary and description of the Westchester architecture.

> *The scope of the intentions of developer and architect is obvious, even in The Westchester's incomplete state. Four buildings containing 556 units cover less than 10 percent of the beautifully landscaped site. Two freestanding irregular I-shaped units flank the entrance drive, a divided road that curves around the main landscape feature, a sunken formally designed elliptical garden. Two large connected buildings irregularly arranged around staggered spines were to have been replicated across the main drive. Although only eight stories tall, the blockiness of each brick-covered unit, unrelieved by either bay windows or balconies, gives them a looming appearance. The placement and scale of The Westchester's Limestone ornamental details do little to relieve the powerful effect of the massive blocks. Its stylistic heritage Neo-Georgian, Neo-Tudor, and Neo-Moorish – is composed of the same ingredients as contemporaneous Hollywood movies, opulence with tasteless style.*

The 1940s and 1950s Bring Big Changes

City Investing Purchases the Westchester 1947

On Feb. 25, 1947, after a year of negotiations, City Investing's Realest Corporation acquired the 27.5 acres of land and the existing Westchester buildings from the Dutch syndicate. The sale was recorded in the District records at 3:26 on 27 February 1947 in Liber 8434, folio 64.

The deed provides a brief history of the property since 1930 by stating that the deed is subject to:

1. *Building restriction lines as established and shown on plat recorded in Liber 96 folio 98 of the office of the Surveyor for the District of Columbia;*
2. *Agreement contained in the dedication recorded in Liber 96 folio 98 of the aforesaid Surveyor's Office Records, that the area between said restriction lines and the line of streets shall be subject to the regulations, restrictions and conditions, as expressed in the Act of Congress of May 31, 1900; 31 Statutes at Large, page 249;*
3. *Perpetual right of way for purposes of ingress and egress over the following described part of said land: Beginning for the same on the Southerly line of Cathedral Avenue at a point distant 257.39 feet westerly on the arc of a circle deflecting to the right and having a radius of 791.33 feet; from the West line of 39th Street, and running thence westerly along said line of said Avenue, on the arc of a circle deflecting to the right and having a radius as aforesaid, an arc distance of 90.88 feet; thence South 30 degrees 10 minutes 30 seconds west 859.59 feet; thence South 59 degrees 49 minutes 30 seconds East, 90 feet; thence North 30 degrees 10 minutes 30 seconds East 871.94 feet to the point of beginning;*
4. *Perpetual easement and right of way granted to the Georgetown Gas Light Company by an agreement recorded in Liber 6634, folio 305 of the Land Records of the District of Columbia;*
5. *Right of way for sewer purposes granted to the District of Columbia by deed recorded in Liber 6645, folio 493, another of said Land Records;*
6. *Deed of Trust from Westchester Development Corporation to Clarence Dodge and Martin R. West, Trustees, dated November 21, 1930 and*

>   recorded in Liber 6504, folio 455, one of the Land Records of the District of Columbia;
> 7. Deed of Trust from Westchester Development Corporation to Clarence Dodge and Martin R. West, Trustees, dated October 14, 1931 and recorded in Liber 6605, folio 32, one of the Land Records of said District;
> 8. Agreement between Westchester Development Corporation and Metropolitan Life Insurance Company, dated October 14, 1931 and recorded in Liber 6605, folio 45, one of the Land Records of said District.

On that same day, 25 February, Realest and two trustees, John S. Thompson and Ira S. Hoddinott, both of Newark, N.J. agreed to an Indenture against the purchased property in the name of The Mutual Benefit Life Insurance Company, also of Newark. Realest signed a promissory note for $3,150,000 with an interest rate of 3.5% per annum through 1951 and 4% through the final payment on Dec. 1, 1961. This indenture was recorded, five minutes after the Deed was registered, with the District on 27 Feb. 1947 in Liber 8434, folio 68. On folio 71 we see the purchase price for The Westchester Apartments, Inc. was $4,197,884 (subject to adjustments at the closing).

The very next day, Realist entered into a deed of trust for the property. This deed, Liber 8434, folio 74, provides further insight into the financial side of the transaction: The Westchester Apartments, Inc. received a $600,000 promissory note of deferred purchase money with an interest rate of 2% with a balloon payment on 28 Feb. 1952.

On Feb. 28, City Investing announced plans to expand the existing buildings and install a recreation center, a swimming pool, a restaurant, and a casino.[52] These plans seem to be a reflection of the amenities in Ring's original 1929 plans.

In 1947 Sen. Carl Hayden [D-Arizona] proposed to build a four-lane divided highway, to be called Arizona Avenue, through what is now known as Glover Archbold Park, from Canal Road in Georgetown to Wisconsin Avenue in Friendship Heights – that highway would have gone through part of the 27.5 acres; but it was never built.[53] Arizona Avenue had been shown on earlier maps (Figure 16) in this location but not as a highway. Of course, there is now an Arizona Avenue west of us by about a mile. In 1947 Glover Archbold Park was officially known as **U.S. Government Reservation No. 351-f** and shown on DC maps as **Glover Parkway**.[54]

In 1952 City Investing Corporation imported the impressive Victorian gates and pillars on the Cathedral Avenue entrance to the campus. The gates were from the Copped Hall estate in Essex, England; the main Copped Hall house had been destroyed in an accidental electric fire in 1917.[55] Many people incorrectly attribute the

---

[52] *Evening Star*, Feb. 28, 1947, page A-7
[53] *Evening Star*, Dec. 21, 1947, page 33
[54] 1947 Deed of Trust, Liber 8434 folio 76
[55] http://coppedhalltrust.org.uk/

destruction to World War II German bombing attacks and state that the gates and stone pillars date back to 1760 and are Georgian.

City president Robert Dowling purchased them and had them shipped to Washington; the purchase price and the fee for the 80-ton shipment came to about $14,000, according to a June 1952 article in the *Evening Star*:

Headline: Gates from England at Westchester

A touch of old England in the form of massive baronial iron gates has been added to the main entrance to the Westchester Apartments at 4000 Cathedral Avenue N.W.

With Manager Janusz Ilinski as host, these decorative gates of "pure Georgian" design, were dedicated Thursday afternoon at a reception attended by prominent District officials, business and professional men.

The baronial gates and the two stone pillars on each side date back to 1760. They were discovered in England, on a recent visit by Robert W. Dowling, president of City Investing Co. of New York, which owns the Westchester. He was wandering though Essex, examining the ruins left by the war blitz, when he spied the gates and pillars standing at the entrance to Copped Hall estate. The rest of the estate had been left in ruins.

Mr. Ilinski had been looking about for some Georgian gates for the Westchester, so Mr. Dowling arranged for the shipment of his find. Purchase price and shipping fees came to about $14,000.

Mr. Dowling came here for the dedication ceremony. The shipment, weighing 80 tons, had arrived only recently.

Dowling had them placed at the campus entrance off Cathedral Avenue. The dedication was on Thursday, June 19, 1952.[56] They are marvelous sentries at what is now the Cathedral Avenue entrance to the Westchester campus as can be seen in the photograph below.

---

[56] *Evening Star*, June 21, 1952, page B-4

Figure 18 The Copped Hall Gates at the Westchester

Between the gates there is a delightful fountain with the water pouring out of a lion's head mouth. The Westchester has seasonal plants in the landscaped area in front of the fountain and gates. The fountain and tulips can be seen on the next page, in front of the two rows of cedar trees leading to the sunken garden. The fountain and surround were restored in 2016, after the picture was taken.

The Copped Hall Trust website tells an interesting story about these gates, which Alan Cox, chairman of the Copped Hall Trust, summarized for me:

> *The two sets of grand gates from the entrance forecourt at Copped Hall have been located in Washington USA by strange co-incidence. A Copped Hall Trust supporter found a small article in a local museum indicating that they had been installed at the Westchester. The full height railings associated with these gates have not been found. There was another grand gate, with associated full height railings, at the end of the garden terraces at Copped Hall, which could also have made its way to America. Ex trustee - Gordon Brown - has kindly offered a reward of $1,000 to anyone who can locate these gates and provide us with the details of the present owners.*[57]

The trustees of the Copped Hall estate tell a different story about the gates than was reported in the *Evening Star* back in 1952. Alan Cox provides this history of the gates:[58]

---

[57] Email from Alan Cox to the author dated Dec. 2, 2017
[58] Email from Alan Cox to the author dated Jan. 4, 2017

Figure 19 The Lion's Head Fountain at the Westchester

The gates and their piers were made in 1895 as part of the very expensive improvements to Copped Hall by Mr. E.J. Wythes - an extremely wealthy man. Mr. Wythes died in 1949 and the 4000-acre estate was sold in 1951.

Mr. Dowling purchased them from Bert Crowther an antiques dealer in West London - who stripped numerous country houses for their statues, gates, etc. As you would know, after the Second World War hundreds of country houses were demolished. 1955 was the worst year when one house was destroyed every 2.5 days.

The gates you have are minus their obelisks that sat on top. The small urns, you now have on top, may well have come from the Copped Hall winter-garden - which was also stripped of its decorative elements at the same time as the gates were removed - before being dynamited in 1960.

The following 1910 picture (Figure 20) of the gates is from *Country Life Magazine*[59] – showing one of the Victorian gates *in situ* at Copped Hall. The pyramids atop the pillars are long gone.

---

[59] *Country Life Magazine*, Oct. 29, 1910, pages 610 – 617, provided to the author by Copped Hall Trust.

Figure 20 The Copped Hall Gates at Copped Hall 1910

The Westchester Becomes a Cooperative

In 1953 the Westchester became a cooperative when Realest sold the apartments to the residents but retained the land and the commercial spaces in the buildings. The tenants were facing buying their apartments or moving out of them by 1 November. The prices ranged from $4,000 for an efficiency apartment to $25,600 for a three-bedroom unit.[60]

Dec. 23, 1953, John S. Thompson and Ira S. Hoddinott released Realest from the Feb. 25, 1947 indenture to The Mutual Benefit Life Insurance Company (Liber 8434, folio 68) and the 1953 document was registered with the District and recorded in Liber 10115, folio 597. Six days later Realest signed an indenture to The Mutual Benefit Life Insurance Company for $4,000,000. The secretary of Realest provided a commitment that included: *a restriction on building on the unimproved land to the effect that any building thereon would have to conform to the existing buildings and would be subject to approval of plans by the lender, which approval would not be unreasonably withheld,*

---

[60] *Evening Star*, Oct. 21, 1953, page A-14

and with the further right to release the unoccupied land from the lien of the first mortgage upon payment of $500,000 in reduction of the principal amount...

This was a preliminary step in the sale of the Westchester buildings (not the land) to the Westchester Corporation on the first day of January 1954. The 20-page *participation agreement* between Realest and the Westchester Corporation was registered with the District and can be found in Liber 10118, starting at folio 271. The agreement detailed specifically what was included in the sale and what was not. Attached to the agreement were two interesting documents:

- **Exhibit A:** Agreement for Acquisition of the Westchester (Liber 10118, starting at folio 279). This exhibit places the sales price at $5,400,000.
- **Exhibit B:** Cooperative Apartment Perpetual Use and Equity Contract (Liber 10118, starting at folio 282)

The items not included in the sale were:

- The 153 apartments that had not yet been sold to residents or others.
- The non-residential areas:
    a) Space now used as a drug store, grocery store and valet and laundry
    b) Space now used as an employees' dining room, kitchen store rooms and connecting corridor
    c) Space now used as a main liquor storage room
    d) Space now used as a barber shop, beauty salon, and cocktail lounge
    e) Space now used as a dining room, terrace and kitchen
    f) Space now used as automobile storage garage in northerly portion of westerly building
    g) Space now used as automobile storage garage in westerly portion of westerly building
    h) Space now used as automobile storage garage in the sub-basement of the westerly portion of westerly building

On Jan. 1, 1954, Realest granted and created an Easement Agreement with the Westchester Corporation. This agreement can be found in Liber 10118, folio 232 through 246, among the land records of the District of Columbia. It says, in part:

1. A ground lease was executed simultaneously with the filing of this agreement
2. Realest also simultaneously executed a deed to Westchester for certain buildings and improvements, with certain exceptions (see previous paragraphs)
3. The Westchester grants Realest access to loading docks and parking garages in their buildings relative to use of the commercial spaces

4. The Westchester grants to Realest the right to use certain portions of the land now used as a roadway (very technical descriptions of the specific land are provided)
5. Realest grants to the Westchester the right to use certain portions of the land now used as a roadway (very technical descriptions of the specific land are provided)
6. Realest grants certain light and air easements to the Westchester A Building, described as the *easterly building*; further that the extension of the easterly building, having dimensions of approximately 14.28 feet X 16.57 feet, shall be permitted to remain as long as the easterly building stands
7. The Westchester grants Realest full access to and use of the *non-residential areas* of their buildings

In 1956 Realest proposed building eight 8-story apartment buildings on the vacant land surrounding the four Westchester buildings. The members of the Westchester Cooperative considered purchasing the roughly 16 acres adjacent to their buildings to prevent the proposed construction.[61] In April 1958 the residents of the Westchester went to the Federal District Court to seek an injunction against the building of the proposed 1,000 room "The Towers" building on "their" vacant land. The injunction requested action against Realest and the District Commissioners. The suit charged that the commissioners granted an improper building permit for the structure and said construction would involve elimination of 90 parking spaces plus the end of the sunken garden on their grounds.[62]

When the Westchester bought its land back from City Investing it also acquired ownership of the space for commercial tenants in the buildings. City had leased those spaces to various commercial tenants since purchasing the Westchester in 1947.

The commercial tenants currently include:

- A grocery store
- A valet
- A dining room serving brunch, lunch, and dinner, (at this date) closed temporarily
- A hair salon
- A barbershop
- A realtor

---

[61] *Evening Star*, Oct. 14, 1956, page A-17
[62] *Evening Star*, April 23, 1958, page A-22

The Westchester Cooperative currently owns one plot of land in Square 1805, Lot 800. The District zoning map63 (Figure 21) shows the lot, which is 10.46 acres.

Figure 21 Current DC Zoning Map, Clipping – the Westchester

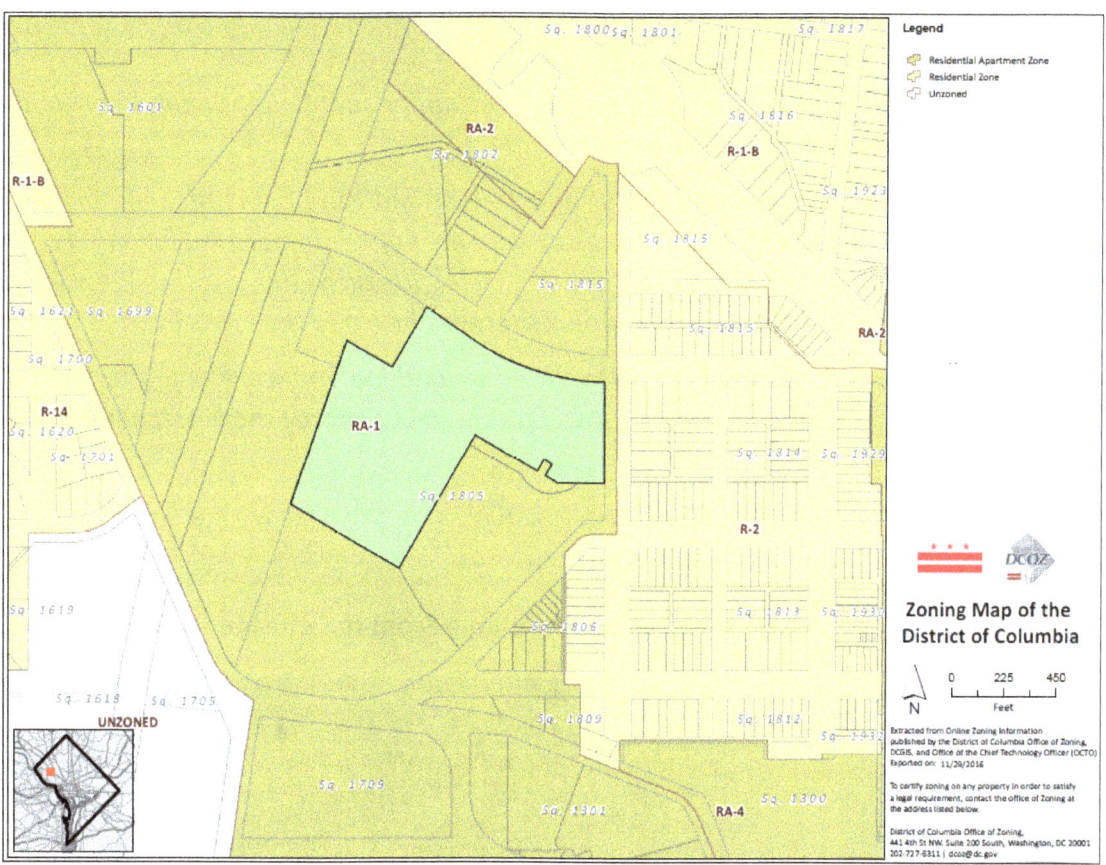

An interesting aspect of the Westchester's history is the number of famous residents, particularly from the political side of town. Many senators, members of the House, Cabinet members, etc. lived here. A very famous Washingtonian, Warren Buffett, didn't live here but delivered newspapers to the Westchester apartments. The story is told in several books and newspaper stories. One nice story about this appeared back on 2 May 2015 in *The Globalsit*, a daily online magazine on the global economy, politics, and culture. Barry Wood interviewed Buffet and reported: [64]

> *Some time back, Buffett told me about his first successful business — delivering newspapers in Washington, DC.*

---

[63] Note that in each of the Zoning Map images (each dated 2016), which follow, there is a vestigial road running up the center of the Glover Archbold Park, a road long planned but never built. Likewise there is a clear trace of the never-built Hamilton Circle.
[64] https://www.theglobalist.com/warren-buffetts-reflections-on-delivering-papers/

Few people are aware that Buffett spent his formative teenage years in Washington, DC, during the time his father was a Member of Congress for six Years

"You learn a lot about human nature when you deliver papers," says Buffett. "For one thing you learn you have to pay for them each month. Whether the customers pay you or not. You have to collect money."

Buffett's family lived in Spring Valley, an upper middle class neighborhood in Washington, not far from the Maryland line.

Buffett says delivering papers at age 14 instilled the importance of hard work and reliability. Wartime Washington was short of adult men and for that reason, says Buffett, he was able to get multiple paper routes at the Westchester Apartments, a five-building complex that was home to the city's elite.

"I also learned," he says, "that if you did a good job you were going to move up. The very fact that I did a good job in Spring Valley got me the Westchester routes later on."

The land that is home to the Westchester COOP is mostly flat with a rolling slope to 39th Street, which can be seen below in Figure 22.

Figure 22 Westchester A Building From the Hillside

The Westchester Gets New Neighbors

Development of 3900 Watson Place

Finally the 27.5 acres start to get subdivided and new construction starts. The first project was City Investing's construction of 3900 Watson Place N.W., a cooperative.

By 1947 City Investing was already leasing and managing the Westchester property. City Investing started another company in 1959, The Eastchester Corporation, to build a cooperative housing project that later became 3900 Watson Place N.W. Inc. Before construction of the double towers of the then Eastchester started, Watson Place, the road, was cut through from the end of Garfield Street to Fulton Street.

Best Addresses does not include 3900 Watson Place directly, but in Chapter 5, "Modernism Reigns Supreme, 1946-1973", there are several mentions of the Watson Place Cooperative and one of its architects, Joseph Able. A few entries from this chapter are worth noting:[65]

- *Most early Washington examples of Modernism were designed by local architects who were noted for their eclectic work, except for Joseph Able and his partners, who tended to combine elements associated with the International Style and streamlined Art Deco.*
- *A notable trend of spacious, park like grounds and large buildings developed, with new apartment houses such as The Rittenhouse, The Towers, 3900 Watson Place, N.W., ..., Watergate, the Colonnade, and the Foxhall.*
- *During the 1950s architects resumed the experimentation of the 1920s with innovative new plans for Washington apartment houses. A good example is 3900 Watson Place, designed in 1959, unusual with eight triangular units per floor in two square-shaped towers.*

In 1959 City's Realest hired Harry Price, New York architect, and, as associate architects, Julian E. Berla and Joseph Henry Able of the eponymous firm, Berla and Able, located at 2000 P St. NW. Less than a year later the first building was completed. These were times when buildings could go from concept to occupancy much faster than today!

---

[65] Goode, James M., *Best Addresses*, chapter 5

The Eastchester Corporation was formally incorporated in Delaware on June 16, 1959. There were three incorporators:

- F. F. Westover
- L. A. Schoonmaker
- A. D. Atwell

The DC government records reflect the issuance of a building permit for both buildings on April 3, 1958 – permit #B-33321. The summary shows Harry Price as well as Berla & Able as the architects but all other records point to a start in 1959 or 1960. The *HistoryQuest DC* web site has an interactive tool for finding the Building Permits. The tool shows the source of the date for Watson Place as "Historical Building Permits Index, Best Addresses". The April 1958 date appears to be a mistake as it is more than a full year before the June 1959 incorporation of the Eastchester.[66]

The stated purpose of the still-existent corporation (albeit under a different corporate name – see next paragraph for the name change) is: *To purchase, or otherwise acquire, operate and manage a single housing project consisting of two buildings and related improvements (hereinafter termed "the project") on a non-profit basis and in the interest and for the housing of its Members and other lawful occupants.*

At 11 a.m. on Feb. 11, 1960, the Eastchester Corporation Board of Directors met and voted to call a special meeting of the board to amend the Certificate of Incorporation, changing the name of the corporation. On March 4, 1960, board members met in a special meeting and five out of the five directors voted in favor of the following amendment to the Certificate of Incorporation: **"The name of the corporation is 3900 WATSON PLACE N. W. INC."**

Currently the name is typically written as *3900 Watson Place* or even *Watson Place* using the street address as the informal name of the cooperative itself. Usually when the full name is used – the "N. W." text is compressed to "N.W."

The directors were:

- R. W. Dowling
- Samuel R. Walker
- John A. Kennedy
- Alfred P. Ileh
- H. F. Noonan[67]

3900 Watson Place currently owns two lots (Large lot 801 & very small lot 802) in Square 1805. Prior to the current record-keeping structure of the District of Columbia the two lots were known as Parcel 31/140 and Parcel 31/138, respectively. The

---

[66] https://dcgis.maps.arcgis.com/apps/webappviewer/index.html?id=4892107c0c5d44789e6fb96908f88f60
[67] 3900 Watson Place N.W. Inc. Certificate of Incorporation, Amendments thereto and By-Laws

District zoning map clipping, on Figure 23 shows the two lots only Lot 801 is shown in green. The total size of the two lots is just slightly larger than 5.5 acres, having 239,782 square feet.[68]

On March 15, 1960, the 3900 Watson Place Board met and set criteria for turning over control to a member-based board. The first annual meeting of 3900 Watson Place was set for Jan. 2, 1961, per the bylaws.

In early June 1960 the first of the two towers at 3900 Watson Place (the B Building) was completed and the second tower was on schedule for completion by 1 July that year.[69] That June 3900 Watson Place started advertisements in the *Evening Star* announcing that the buildings were ready for occupancy.[70] The sales brochure stated that there were *152 two bedroom-two bath apartment units*. There were 68 units in the A Building and 84 in the B Building. All but a few units in each building have a balcony or a ground-level terrace. Additionally there were 133 indoor parking spaces in the underground, two-story parking garage. The garage has a *green roof*, with a lawn and plantings, which forms part of the lawn between the buildings and in front of the B Building.

Figure 23 Current DC Zoning Map, Clipping – 3900 Watson Place

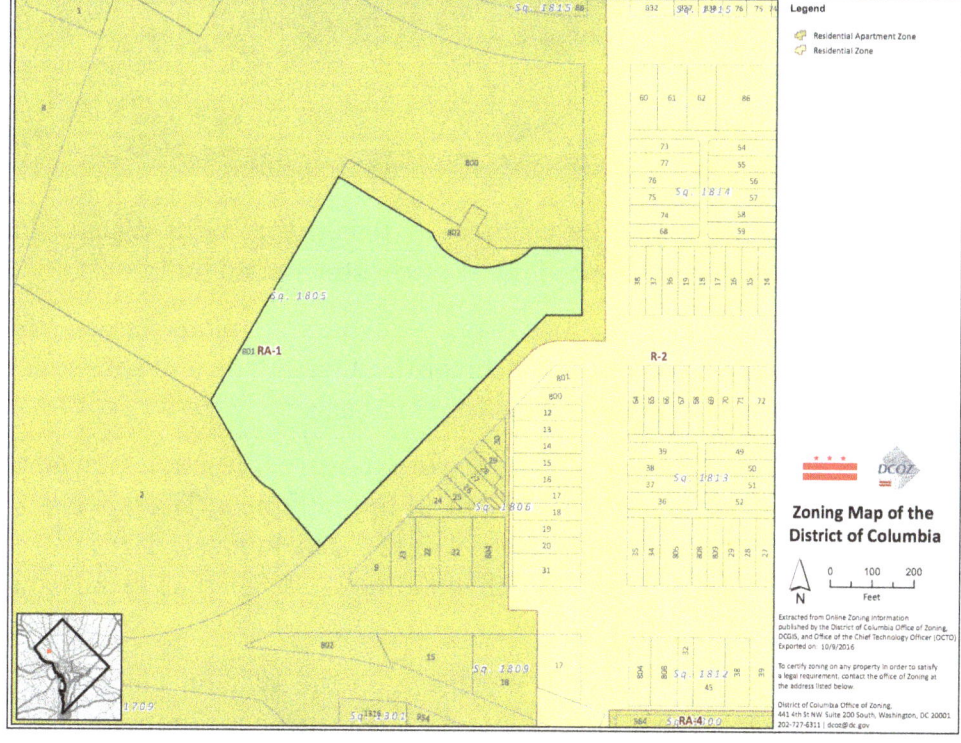

---

[68] Ground lease granted by Realest Corporation to 3900 Watson Place N.W. Washington, DC, dated 18 December 1962 and recorded in Liber 11925, folio 441, of the land records of the District of Columbia
[69] *Evening Star*, June 4, 1960, page B-9
[70] *Evening Star*, July 1, 1960, page A-2

The B Building and the lawn over the underground garage can be seen in Figure 24.

Figure 24 The 3900 Watson Place B Building and Lawn

The view above is taken from the roadway between the 3900 Watson Place's B Building and the *Cedar Allie* in front of the Westchester's main building.

The sales brochure featured the occupant – ownership plan: "under this plan, occupants become owners of Use Contracts for the apartments and consequently are in a position to preserve the highest dwelling standards."

The sales prices were based on a combination of exposure (direction viewed from the terrace and the windows) as well as height in the buildings. There were 12 price points starting at $25,440 and going up to $38,160. The highest prices were for the four units on the 8th floor (two in each building: A & B) that faced southwest, specifically Units A8B, A8C, B8B, and B8C.

On July 21, 1960, Realest took out a mortgage on the Watson Place property for $3,000,000. The lender was the Mutual Benefit Life Insurance Company.

By that October there were two advertisements for 3900 Watson Place:

1. A small classified advertisement for a two-bedroom, two-bath unit in an *Attractive Location* – 3900 Watson Place. The advertisement described

the *Co-Operative* as offering *"Country Estate Atmosphere in the Heart of the City."* It went on to boast of *"a spectacular view of the Potomac River and the Virginia Hills from Washington's Most Beautiful Vantage Point."*[71]

2. A large advertisement for 3900 Watson Place, with a picture, touting "Washington's newest and most desirable Co-Operative – now being occupied.[72] See the text in Figure 26.

Figure 25 1960 Advertisement for 3900 Watson Place

> WASHINGTON'S NEWEST AND MOST DESIRABLE
> # CO-OPERATIVE
> NOW BEING OCCUPIED
>
> BEAUTIFULLY LANDSCAPED GROUNDS IN THE HEART OF THE CITY
>
> A SPECTACULAR VIEW OF THE POTOMAC RIVER AND THE VIRGINIA HILLS
>
> TWO BEDROOM, TWO BATH SPACIOUSNESS
> EACH APARTMENT HAS ITS OWN BALCONY.
> INDIVIDUAL FINGERTIP CONTROL OF HEATING
> AND AIR-CONDITIONING IN EACH ROOM.
> ALL-ELECTRIC KITCHEN, DISHWASHER, DISPOSAL
>
> AGENT ON PREMISES • TELEPHONE FEDERAL 8-7770 • SALES OFFICE OPEN 10 A M TO 8 P M EVERY DAY INCLUDING SUNDAY

As stated in the advertisement, the views are truly spectacular. From the roof of the Watson Place A Building, once can see the Potomac River, Reagan Airport, and a hint of the Memorial Bridge. The view from the top floor of Building A, looking at the National Cathedral, is also quite spectacular (Figure 26).

---

[71] *Sunday Star*, Oct. 23, 1960, page E-10
[72] Sunday Star 23 Oct. 1960, page H-3

Figure 26 View of the National Cathedral From the A Building

By early 1961 the advertisements for 3900 Watson Place featured the theme of *Gracious living unlimited ... in the Nation's Capital*.[73] Some of the advertisement can be seen in Figure 27.

---

[73] *Washington Star*, Feb. 17, 1961, page B-5

Figure 27 1961 Advertisement of Watson Place Services

Ownership of an apartment home at 3900 Watson Place, N.W., means more than possession of just four walls—it is **Gracious Living Unlimited**. In addition to a beautifully designed terraced apartment in a quiet country estate atmosphere in the heart of Washington, it means personal services never before offered with Co-operative apartment ownership.

THE SERVICES: Our special services office will assist you in making arrangements for:

Household Help: A maid, cook, or butler for a day, week, month, or for a special occasion.

Baby-Sitters: A qualified baby-sitter.

Limousine Service: A chauffeured limousine for the length of time desired.

Ticket Service: To sporting events and theatre.

DINING: A direct telephone line has been set up between 3900 Watson Place and the fashionable Westchester Dining Room—just a step from 3900 Watson Place. This line may be used to make Dining Room reservations or to request catering service in your apartment.

At 11 a.m. on Aug. 31, 1962, the 3900 Watson Place Board of Directors met and voted to call a special meeting to amend the Certificate of Incorporation, the 8th Amendment. On Sept. 17, 1962, the board members met in that special meeting and five out of the five directors voted in favor of the following amendment to the Certificate of Incorporation: *The management of the affairs of the corporation shall be conducted in accordance with the requirements of its by-laws. During the first four* years of the corporate existence, the board of directors shall have the power and authority to make, alter and amend the by-laws of the corporation: thereafter the power and authority to make, alter and amend the by-laws shall vest in the membership and on such terms and with such delegated rights in the*

Directors shall be expressed in the by-laws. ... Four more paragraphs were included in the eighth amendment.

* Amended by raising "two," in the original, to "four."[74]

The directors of 3900 Watson Place were all employees of City Investing / Realest:

- R. W. Dowling
- Samuel R. Walker
- Forrest Leonard Daniels
- Howard F. Noonan
- Hazel T. Bowers

Later in 1962 the board of directors notified the owners that they had to pay the balance of the equity cost of their apartments on or before Dec. 24, 1962. The original down payment was 33% of the unit sales price. But initially purchasers were able to pay 10% of this amount as a cooperative apartment *deposit.* Now the board required a full payment of the down payment. If owners elected to not pay the rest of the down payment, they could elect to receive back their 10% deposit per the Cooperative Apartment Deposit Agreement. There is no record of owners using this exit option. This requirement for full down payments was no doubt driven by Realest advising the board of 3900 Watson Place that it was *definitely determined to transfer the project to the Cooperative at settlement on Dec. 28, 1962.* The announcement went on to say: *Thereafter, Realest Corporation, we are informed, desires that the project be operated primarily for the happiness and satisfaction of all members of the Cooperative.*[75]

> *Realest Corporation desires that the project be operated primarily for the happiness and satisfaction of all members of the Cooperative.*

In December 1962 there were two significant transactions between Realest and 3900 Watson Place N.W. Inc. They were both to be effective on Dec. 31 that year.

1. Realest deeded the two buildings and the improvements (the two buildings and the underground parking tower between the two buildings) to 3900 Watson Place N.W. Inc. The deed to the buildings is in Libor 11925, folio 505, at the DC Register of Deeds.
2. Realest leased the land, which today is the property of the 3900 Watson Place N.W. Inc. to the cooperative. The 57-page deed is known as a

---

[74] Certificate of Amendment of 3900 WATSON PLACE N.W. Certificate of Incorporation
[75] Announcement by Samuel R. Walker, president, 3900 Watson Place (not dated)

ground lease (but often referred to as a land lease) as it does not refer to the buildings and improvements other than to say they are not included and that the lessor has an obligation to maintain them. This ground lease is in Libor 11925, folios 439 through 495 at the DC Register of Deeds. Some highlights of the ground lease:
a) The start date of the ground lease was noon on Dec. 31, 1962
b) The end date of the ground lease was noon on Dec. 31, 2061
c) The rent was to be paid in equal monthly installments in the amount of $50,000 per annum
d) Watson Place was responsible for taxes, maintenance, and upkeep of the buildings and other improvements
e) The perpetual use contracts were to include language passing the ground lease obligations to members; a specifically worded <u>Co-operative Apartment Perpetual Use and Equity Contract</u> was an attachment to the ground lease

At that point Watson Place assumed the existing (July 1960) first mortgage with Mutual Benefit Life Insurance Co. with an outstanding balance of $2,818,986.63 as of the Feb. 28, 1963 balance sheet. Watson Place also assumed a Second Trust with Realest with an outstanding balance of $466,357.87 as of the 28 February 1963 balance sheet. Further Realest was issued a Perpetual Use and Equity Contract for each unsold unit and agreed to make the associated monthly payments for each of these units.

The 1964 budget figures were dominated by: a first trust with a payment in the amount of $240,000; a second trust with a payment in the amount of $24,000; and a ground lease with Realest with a $50,000 payment to be prorated across the 12 months. The total of those three disbursements was $314,000 out of a budget of $532,988 or 59% of the budget.

On Sept. 29, 1964, the Owners Committee was pushing to convert 3900 Watson Place from a cooperative to a condominium. At this point the activation of the cooperative required 80% of the units to be *sold* and that milestone had not yet been reached. However, the record shows that effective with the Dec. 31, 1962 transfer of the buildings to 3900 Watson Place that a cooperative had been legally established, but there was some question about the IRS tax benefits prior to the 80% mark. The Owners Committee employed the services of Murray, Nobiletti, & Kenny, Attorneys and Counselors at Law at One Rockefeller Plaza in New York City. On that September date the law firm wrote a two-page proposal relative to the conversion to the member-owners of 3900 Watson Place N.W. Inc. There is no record that the proposal was put to a vote at a "Special Meeting", per the By-laws.

As of Jan. 1, 1965, Realest still owned the 64 apartment units not yet sold, out of 152 (42%); many of them were rented out by Realest. Realest paid rent to the Cooperative for one garage space for each of the 64 units as well as monthly fees for each unit they owned; where the unit was rented out the renters paid the $20 monthly parking fee and their monthly unit fees.[76]

In the summer of 1965 apartments were advertised in the 3900 Watson Place buildings – one-, two-, and three-bedroom apartments as well as double units with three or more bedrooms. The monthly charges for a two-bedroom unit were $242.44.[77]

On Sept. 30, 1965, the 3900 Watson Place board met in NYC and further implemented the cooperative plan by electing six members to the board from the *Advisory Board of Owners*. Their service was to be effective at the Jan. 3, 1966, annual meeting to be held in the Watson Place G2-level garage at 8 p.m.

By Jan. 10, 1966, the requisite 80% of the units had been sold, but Realist still owned about 30 units. On that date the first 3900 Watson Place board meeting was held with owner-members rather than just City Investing and Realest members. My father was a member of the board as he represented City Investing's Realest Corporation, which held the ground lease, a second trust, and owned several empty and rented apartments in the two buildings.

On 27 April 1966 Realest sold the land where 3900 Watson Place is (parcels 31/140 and 31/138) to the Ohio Teachers Reality Corporation (later known as the Teachers Realty Corporation). This deed was recorded with the District in Liber 12601, folio 572.

On Feb. 14, 1972, the annual meeting of the membership was held in the Westchester's dining room. The approved budget for 1972 was presented. The highlights:

- Overall budget $647,500
- $119,000 salaries and wages
- $49,000 electricity
- $69,950 real estate taxes
- $50,000 ground lease

On March 1, 1980, City Investing Corporation and 3900 Watson Place mutually agreed and signed that the second deed and note were fully paid. According to the April 2, 1980, Watson Place Members Newsletter, reaching this agreement involved considerable work, particularly on the part of John Wilson, B7BC, chair of the Legal Affairs Committee.

On Feb. 24, 1987, 3900 Watson Place purchased, from Teachers Realty Corporation (formerly known as the Ohio Teachers Realty Corporation), the land under our

---

[76] Watson Place NW, Inc. budget estimate for 1965, Dec 17, 1964
[77] *Evening Star*, June 4, 1965, page C-3

buildings and the vacant land around them. At that point the ground lease was terminated and the deed releasing 3900 Watson Place from that lease was registered with the District.[78]

Like the Westchester, over the years 3900 Watson Place has had its fair share of well-known residents – many from the political side of town as well as from the arts. One such resident made the March 14, 1949 cover of *TIME* - Perle Mesta.

It was Mesta's appointment as Ambassador to Luxembourg (1949-1953) that inspired Irving Berlin's hit musical *Call Me Madam*, starring Ethel Merman as the famous socialite. During the 1950s Mesta remained Washington's premier hostess as the informal charm and gaiety of her entertaining attracted the cream of international society.[79] She was referred to in the press as the *hostess with the mostest*.

When 3900 Watson Place opened she lived in a large, four-unit apartment (units B8A, B8B, B8C, & B8H) on the 8th floor of the B Building. The combined units had their own marble foyer and she was given free rent by Realest as a marketing move. Five years later, when the buildings became cooperatives she refused to pay any rent or purchase the units.

As vice president of Realest, my dad was asked to intervene. He told me that when he called her, she asked him, *"Do you know who I am?"* My father responded. *"Yes, you are the lady who refuses to pay her rent."* He said they were able to work together after that opening volley, eventually reaching an amicable agreement as can be seen in a letter (Figure 28), which Mesta sent him in September 1966.

In 1967 when Mesta moved out of Watson Place the *Washington Star* ran a gossip column item, *Your Date with Ymelda*, proving the value of the marketing decision to not charge Mesta rent:

> *Perle Mesta is leaving 3900 Watson Place, the address she made famous because she lived and entertained there.*
>
> *The Johnson family have all visited there, so have the Humphreys, senators, representatives, Cabinet members, cave dwellers, movie and stage greats, plus military mighty.*[80]

---

[78] District Registrar Liber 22900, folio 660.
[79] www.britanica.com/biography/perle-Mesta.
[80] *Evening Star*, July 6, 1967, page 37

Figure 28 Perle Mesta Letter

> PERLE S. MESTA
>
> Washington, D. C.
> September 17, 1966
>
> Mr. Joseph A. Higgins, Vice President
> Realest Corporation
> 980 Madison Avenue
> New York 21, N. Y.
>
> Dear Mr. Higgins:
>
> Thank you for your letter of September 15, 1966 in which you enclosed an agreement in duplicate copies covering Apartment 8A, B, C & H, "B" Building, 3900 Watson Place, N. W., Washington, D. C. I have signed both and will return to you herewith the original and retain the executed copy for my file.
>
> I appreciate your kind offer to help in any way possible when I vacate the apartment and I am pleased that we were able to reach the agreement.
>
> Sincerely yours,
>
> Perle Mesta

After she moved out of Watson Place she settled into luxurious space at the Sheraton Park apartments. An article in the Society-Home section of the Aug. 20, 1967 *Sunday Star*, (page E-2) described the new apartment with references to her Watson Place address.

> *When Mrs. Perle Mesta throws her first party in her new Sheraton Park apartment guests will have the pleasant feeling they have been there before.*
>
> *In fact it will seem as if her old penthouse apartment at 3900 Watson Place NW had been transplanted to the new location–complete with Rock Creek Park view.*
>
> *That's because every detail of it will be like the Watson Place apartment she has occupied for the last five-years and which she would not be vacating "if it hadn't gone cooperative."*

Development of the Colonnade

The Colonnade is located at 2801 New Mexico Ave. NW; it is in Square 1805, Lot 0002. The District zoning map below shows the lot. The total size of the lot is 7.5 acres, with the Colonnade building covering about two of those acres.[81]

Figure 29 Current DC Zoning Map, Clipping – the Colonnade

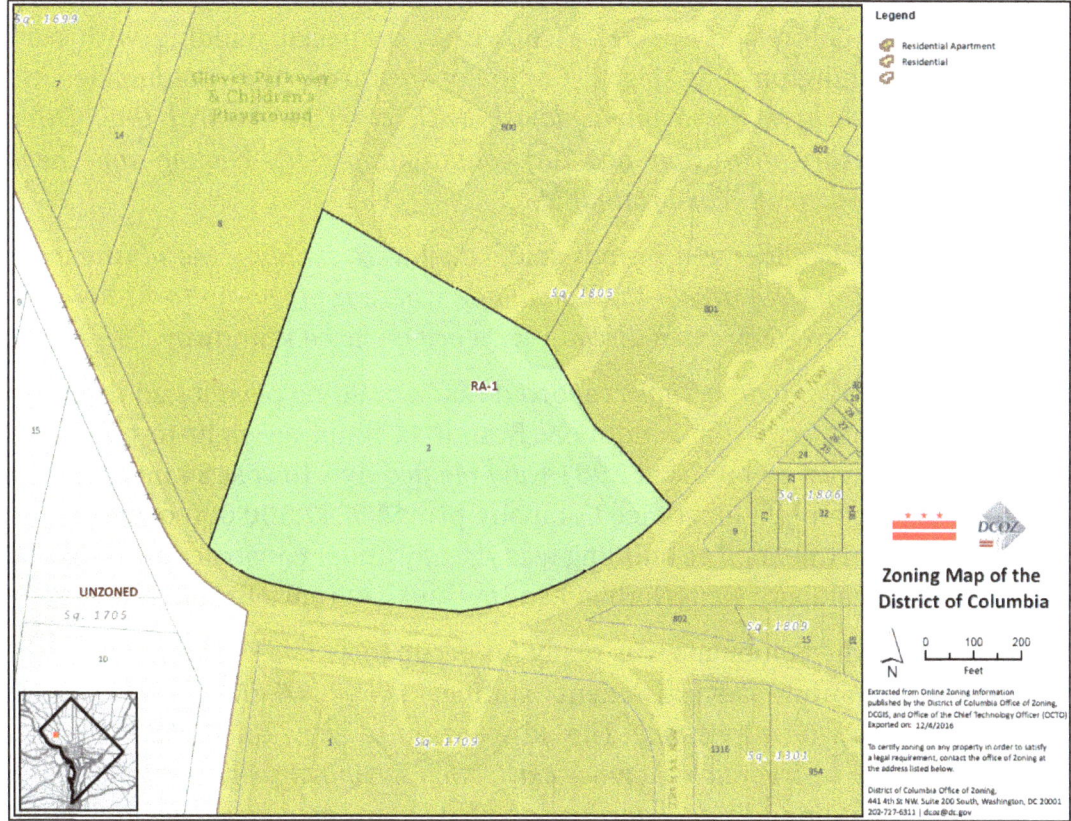

On 30 October 1963 Realest sold a parcel of land to be developed by the purchasers. They eventually sold two more parcels to other developers for the same general purpose. This parcel was sold to the following persons, as joint tenants:

- Nathan Landow
- Lawrence Brandt
- Wiley T. Buchanan, Jr.[82]

---

[81] Goode, James M., *Best Addresses*, page 462
[82] DC Registrar Liber 12102, folio 421

Landow and Brandt were well-known local builders. Founded in 1959 as a family-owned business, Landow & Company is now recognized as one of the largest privately-held real estate development firms located in the Greater Washington, D.C. Metropolitan Area. Landow & Company's services encompass all phases of real estate development, including land acquisition, financing, site planning and development, building design, construction, leasing and asset and property management. The company's web site lists 18 luxury apartment projects, four major office-building developments, various retail developments, and the Dulles Jet Center, the largest aircraft hangar based facility in the nation.[83] The list includes the Colonade (sic) as one of their projects and has what appears to be an architect's rendering of the building rather than an actual image.

In late 1964 the Colonnade opened a showcase, a special building with sample apartments. Washington Gas Light Company featured the Colonnade in an advertisement – *"where the living is lavish with carefree natural GAS! Offering incredible new luxury, featuring gas air conditioning with cooling and heating controlled in each room all year-around!"*[84]

By February 1965 Landow and Brandt said, *"they were building the most expensive building in the entire (DC) area – the Colonnade where rents go up to $1,900 for the penthouse – and we're 70% rented already, with occupancy a year away."* [85]

In April 1965 the *Washington Times* reported that a building permit had been issued to Lawrence Brandt et al. for Landow & Brandt to build an eight-to-twelve-story apartment house with 274 units at 2901 New Mexico Ave. to cost $4 million.[86] Later in 1965 Metropolitan Life Insurance Company provided $7,500,000 of financing for the Colonnade Apartments. The building was already under construction at that point. The builders / developers were Nathan Landow and Lawrence Brandt.[87]

By summer 1966 the Colonnade was ready for occupancy. The Washington Gas Light Company ran another advertisement stating, *"NOW OPEN … NEW MODEL APARTMENTS open for inspection."* The ad went on to say: *"Only when you see the Colonnade, will you believe such elegance exists! In a setting of six park-like acres you'll find sparkling fountains, fairytale gardens and formal promenades. The opulent lobby matches your most extravagant dreams. Shopping, parking, swimming, and a host of services are at your command."*[88]

---

[83] http://landowco.com/
[84] *Sunday Star*, Dec. 13, 1964, page A-2
[85] *Evening Star*, Feb. 19, 1965, page D-1
[86] *Evening Star*, Apr. 23, 1965, page F-5
[87] *Evening Star*, March 8, 1965, page A-19
[88] *Sunday Star*, July 31, 1966, page A-2

Figure 30 Colonnade Front Lawn and Trees

The architect was Donald Hudson Drayer, AIA, and the engineering firm was Shefferman & Bigelson. In the Library of Congress's *Donald H. Drayer Archive* there is a collection of 218 items that includes the following Colonnade related items:

- Architectural drawings,
- Structural drawings
- Electrical systems drawings
- Mechanical systems drawings
- Renderings
- Landscape architecture drawings
- Topographic maps
- As-built drawings

The building originally had 283 apartments (more than the earlier announced design) and was a mixture of 24 efficiencies, 137 one-bedroom, 109 two-bedroom, and 13 three-bedroom configurations. Each unit had a balcony and there was valet parking. The Colonnade offers many amenities to the residents, to include: *a 24-hour concierge, doormen, valet, recreation room, dry cleaner, beauty shop, fitness center, sauna, and a large heated swimming pool with landscaped terraces and cabanas.*[89] The lobby, like that of the Cathedral West, is largely glass enclosed.

As described in *Best Addresses*, "*the Colonnade resembles an elegant resort hotel. The grounds are exceptionally well planned.*" Robert Frost designed the grounds. Figure 30 shows the beautiful lawn, trees, and plantings.

In 1973 a feature in the *Evening Star* on condominiums in the Washington area mentioned the Colonnade (and the Cathedral West). A couple of interesting facts about the Colonnade were in the article:

- *When the Shoreham West and the Cathedral West went to condominiums, many who elected not to purchase their units moved to the luxury apartment house – the Colonnade.*
- *The Colonnade, which offers indoor and outdoor swimming, shops, restaurants, a grocery store, and a beauty shop, offers rentals from $350 for a one-bedroom apartment.*
- *The top luxury rentals in the District are the Colonnade and the Towers.*[90]

The article goes on to report that starting in 1961, after Congress passed a law permitting states to approve ownership of a housing unit without the owner holding title to the land on which it rests, condominiums sprung up in many places. In 1963 the District passed a law permitting condominiums.[91] This impacted how our neighborhood and many parts of the City evolved.

Goode reports that right after Landow and Brandt sold the Colonnade to Stuart Bernstein and John Mason in 1974 for more than $15 million, plans were made to convert the Colonnade to a condominium. That July the District government approved the conversion. Approximately half the residents purchased their apartments.[92]

The story is more complex than a simple sale.

- Back in November 1967 Landow, W-D Associates (the Partnership), and the Trustees of the Pennsylvania Real Estate Investment Trust (PREIT) established a co-owners' agreement on joint ownership. The agreement was recorded in Liber 12823, folio 9.
- 21 June 1974 the signatories to the co-owners' agreement signed a new agreement that removed all of the covenants to the property since they had all sold their interests in the property.
- 15 June 1974 Landow and his wife Barbara Landow (parties of the first part), the trustees of PREIT (parties of the second part), the partners of

---

[89] https://colonnadedc.com/amenities
[90] Horwitz, Elinor Lander, "Condominium Craze," *Evening Star*, May 27, 1973, page 173
[91] ibid
[92] Goode, James M., *Best Address*, page 465

W-D Associates (parties of the third part) – all three parties forming the grantors; and The Colonnade Associates (the party of the fourth part) known as the grantee all signed a deed[93] that granted and conveyed the Colonnade (land & buildings) to the Grantee.

The building is quite striking, as can be seen in the photograph from Fulton Street – Figure 31. The Colonnade's large, outdoor swimming pool is directly behind the fence. The roof of the cabana can be seen in the picture.

Figure 31 Exterior Image of the Colonnade

[93] DC Registrar Deed Liber 15745

Development of the Cathedral West

The Cathedral West is located at 4100 Cathedral Ave. NW. It is in Square 1805, Lot 0001. The following District zoning map below shows the lot. The total size of the lot is 2.5 acres. The map also shows the never built Glover Parkway and the Children's Playground.

Figure 32 Current DC Zoning Map, Clipping – the Cathedral West

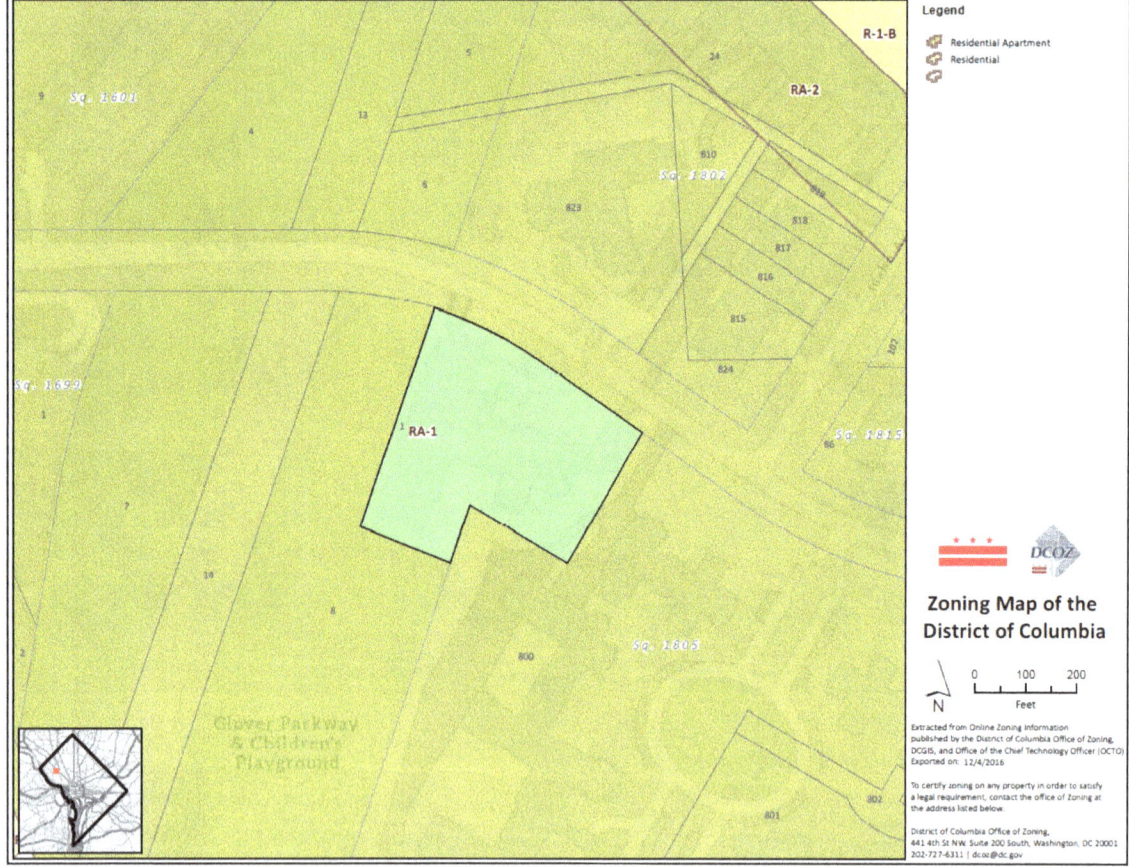

On 27 May 27 1964, Realist conveyed the land where the Cathedral West is now located to three men as joint tenants:

- Donald A. Brown
- Joseph A. Gildenhorn
- Gerald J. Miller[94]

---

[94] DC Registrar Liber 12225, folio 91

The three men had a law practice, Miller, Brown & Gildenhorn, at 1101 17th St. NW at that time. Around this time they stopped practicing law and became real estate developers and financiers; they started doing business as (DBA) MBG Associates.

That 1964 deed referred to a 1954 easement agreement, as follows:

> WHEREAS, by Deed dated May 27, 1964, recorded in Liber 12225, at folio 91, of the land records of the District of Columbia, Realest conveyed certain land to said joint tenants reciting that the land thereby conveyed was subject to a certain right of way and easement and conditions as set forth in an Easement Agreement dated January 1, 1954, recorded at Liber 10118, at folio 232, and described said easement as including certain land by metes and bounds containing a record area of 1,843 square feet and an actual measured area of 2,012 square feet;

On July 31, 1964, the three parties having an interest in the larger piece of land, which the deed reflected the sale of only a portion, signed a supplemental easement agreement as questions had arisen about the accuracy of the 1954 agreement. The revised agreement was registered with the District of Columbia and can be found in Liber 12254, folio 578. The parties were:

- Donald A. Brown, Joseph A. Gildenhorn, and Gerald J. Miller, joint tenants, parties of the first part, hereinafter called "grantors,"
- Realest Corporation, a corporation organized under the laws of the State of New York, party of the second part, hereinafter called "Realest," and
- The Westchester Corporation, a corporation organized under the laws of the State of Delaware, party of the third part, hereinafter called "cooperative,"

This supplemental agreement mentions a term-limited ground lease (referred to as a *certain lease*) from Realist to the Westchester Corporation (referred to as the cooperative), as follows:

> AND WHEREAS, questions have arisen concerning the validity of the description contained in said Deed of May 27, 1964, which the parties hereto desire to correct by this Supplemental Agreement and to create hereby an easement over and upon said land of a recorded area of 1,843 square feet and an actual measured area of 2,012 square feet for the remainder of a term of a certain lease from Realest to the Cooperative dated as of January 1, 1954, and recorded in Liber 10118, folio 165, among the land records of the District of Columbia, and any renewal or extension thereof; ...

That July 20 the DC Board of Zoning Adjustment held a public hearing. One topic on the agenda was a request by Donald A. Brown, et al, an appeal to the board for permission *to erect an apartment building with roof structures in accordance with Section 3308 of the Zoning Regulations at 4100 Cathedral Avenue, N.W., lot 1, Square*

1805. The reference to *an office building* in the appeal decision document is clearly wrong.

The appeal was granted for the following reasons:

> 1) *From the records and the evidence adduced at the hearing, the Board finds that the enclosure on the roof of this proposed office building for service equipment will harmonize with the main structure in architectural character, material and color.*
> 2) *There was no objection to the granting of this appeal registered at the public hearing.*[95]

19 Jan. 1965, was the start of an interesting transfer of the Cathedral West property:

- Brown, Gildenhorn and Miller sold a parcel of land (Parcel 31, lot 133) to a Frances W. Alspach – Liber 12351, folio 554.
- Frances W. Alspach sold the same parcel to Brown, Gildenhorn, Miller, and Harry Lenkin, Melvin Lenkin, and Lawrence Lenkin – Liber 12351, folio 557.
- On 2 Feb that year, Brown, Gildenhorn, Miller, and the Lenkins signed an indenture trust committing the parcel to the Cathedral West Associates who had supplied the consideration for the purchase – Liber 12557, folio 443.

In July 1965 the Evening Star Real Estate Section ran a story on the Cathedral West, reporting: "Competing in the super-deluxe category with such current apartment projects as the Watergate and the Colonnade will be a much smaller apartment house, Cathedral West, on which construction was begun recently at 4100 Cathedral Avenue. NW."[96]

The article went on to identify the builder, the Lenkin Company, and the management company, MBG Properties. The Lenkin Company still builds and manages buildings in the DC area – having started in 1929. The funding, $3 million, for Cathedral West was provided by the Riggs National Bank and the Prudential Insurance Company of America.

The architect, J. Allan MacLane, and the builder agreed to leave the natural slope of the land alone and to preserve as many trees as possible. The slope dictated that the building range in height from three to six stories. The small stream in front of the building was not put into a pipe but rather a small bridge was designed as part of the entrance into the lobby and the garage areas as shown in Figure 33. The bridge leads

---

[95] Order of the Board of Zoning Adjustment, DC, dated April 20, 1965
[96] "Cathedral West to Offer Atriums", *Evening Star*, July 2, 1965, page C-2

into a courtyard with two fountains in it. In the second picture (Figure 34) the bridge can clearly be seen from the side; when the picture was captured, the stream was dry.

Figure 33 Bridge Leading to the Cathedral West

Figure 34 Side View of the Cathedral West Bridge

Figure 35 Cathedral West Fountains

On Jan. 1, 1966, the *Evening Star* reported that the District issued a building permit back in 1965 for the construction of a six-story concrete and brick apartment building with 94 units at 4100 Cathedral Ave. at a cost of $1 million. The permit was issued to Donald A. Brown et al, owner; it identified the builder as Pennsylvania House Construction Co. and the architect as MacLane & Chewning.

Construction started that January. On Jan. 12, 1966, (and numerous other days that month) there was an advertisement in the *Evening Star* for bricklayers to report to numerous locations, including 4100 Cathedral Ave. The pay was $5.25 per hour; work was for a 6-day week with time and a half over 40 hours. The advertisement was placed by the A. Izzo Co., Inc.[97] This now-defunct company registered with the DC Government on May 19, 1961, as Anthony Izzo Co. Inc.[98]

On Feb. 2, 1966, the trustees transferred the project to The Cathedral West Associates, a partnership. The transfer was performed via a trust agreement filed with the District Register of Deeds in Liber 12557, folio 443.

In December 1966 the Cathedral West apartments opened and offered not only a 24-hour doorman and secretarial service but also valet parking. There were two parking

---

[97] *Evening Star*, Jan. 13, 1966, page C-4
[98] https://www.bizapedia.com/dc/anthony-izzo-co-inc.html

spaces for each of the 90 apartments. The *Evening Star* quotes the apartment developer as saying, *"The most expensive apartment house in town and the best. ..."*[99]

A month after the opening the *Evening Star* had an article on the amenities to include the *unusual atrium units*; in fact, the headline was: *Cathedral West has Unusual Atrium Units*. Some highlights mentioned include:

- Indoor-outdoor pool, glass enclosed and heated in the winter and open to the sun and breezes in summer
- There are 17 atrium penthouse apartments. The atriums, open to the sky, for the cores of the living rooms, which are otherwise glassed in.
- Each master bedroom has a dressing room with built-in vanity table and sink.
- Most apartments have four or five walk-in closets.
- Kitchens have walk-in pantries and double sinks.[100]

Interestingly, the builder, Harry A. Lenkin, and the architect, J. Allan MacLane, both died within 16 months of the opening of the Cathedral West apartments. Both of their obituaries mentioned the Cathedral West apartments as examples of their quality work during their lifetimes.

- Lenkin died on 25 April 1967 at Doctors Hospital. His obituary listed him as being 68 years old and reported that he was a member of Washington Post No. 58, Jewish War Veterans. Lenkin was brought to America from Europe as a boy. In 1933 he and his brother, Morris Lenkin, started The Lenkin Construction Company.[101]
- MacLane died on 15 March 1968 at Sibley Memorial Hospital. His obituary listed him as being 43 years old and went on to say he had joined the army in 1943 and fought in the Pacific Theater in WW II. After the war he earned a bachelor of architecture degree from Catholic University.[102]

On April 28, 1967, the *Evening Star* had a photograph of the Cathedral West's indoor swimming pool with the caption: A Pool for All Seasons. *It went on to say that Cathedral West, a new 96-unit apartment building at 4100 Cathedral Ave. NW, has opened a glass-enclosed, indoor-outdoor swimming pool that is heated in the winter and open to the sun in the summer.*[103] The pool enclosure can be seen at the rear of the building – see Figure 36.

---

[99] "Cathedral West Has Unusual Atrium Units," *Evening Star*, Jan. 20, 1967, page G-11
[100] *Evening Star*, Jan. 20, 1967, page G-11
[101] *Evening Star*, April 27, 1967, page B-5
[102] *Sunday Star*, 17 March 1968, page B-14
[103] *Evening Star*, April 28, 1927, page D-2

Figure 36 Cathedral West Swimming Pool Enclosure

By the summer of 1972 penthouse apartments in the Cathedral West (now identified as a condominium) were being advertised in the newspaper as part of the conversion to a condominium. Either one-bedroom plus den or two-bedroom models were advertised as being available in *Washington's most luxurious condominium* for $54,600.[104] By that December the prices included a two-bedroom penthouse offered for $83,000.[105]

In 1973 an *Evening Star* feature on condominiums in the Washington area mentioned the Cathedral West (and the Colonnade apartments). A couple of interesting facts about the Cathedral West were in the article:

- When the small luxury apartment house Cathedral West was converted to a condominium, the syndicate, which had constructed the building five years previously, reportedly made a splendid profit on the deal.
- When the Cathedral West was converted, a committee of tenants brought in a lawyer and engineer and gave the owners a list of changes they wanted made, such as redecoration of public spaces. Ultimately, 55 percent of the apartments were sold to former tenants. The rest were sold within three months with almost no advertising.

---

[104] *Evening Star*, Aug. 23, 1972, page 75
[105] *Evening Star*, 17 Dec. 17, 1972, page 53

- Many renters who elected not to buy moved to the Colonnade, which at the time had no plan *to go condominium*.
- The apartments sold for an average price of $40 per square foot.[106]

The signage for the Cathedral West Condominium is crisp and modern as well as backlit – see Figure 37.

Figure 37 Cathedral West Signage

---

[106] Horwitz, Elinor Lander, "Condominium Craze", *Evening Star*, May 27, 1973, page 173

Development of the Ginger Elkins Subdivision

In August 1967 Ginger Elkins purchased the land on the south side of Watson Place NW from the Realest Corporation for a down payment of $59,000. These lots, prior to the subdivision, were formerly known as Lot 10 in Square 1806. This land was separated from the rest of the original 27.5 acres when the street named Watson Place NW was built. Elkins purchased the land for the development of townhouses. This sale completed Realest Corporations subdividing of the larger tract of land that Ring has assembled in the 1930 time period.

The land consisted of seven vacant lots numbered 24 through 30 in Square 1806, as per the plat recorded in Liber 152, at folio 183, in the Office of the Surveyor for the District of Columbia. The District zoning map (Figure 38) shows the seven lots (Note: to generate the map a single address has to be selected. I chose lot 24, an end unit.)

Figure 38 Current DC Zoning Map, Clipping – Ginger Elkins Subdivision

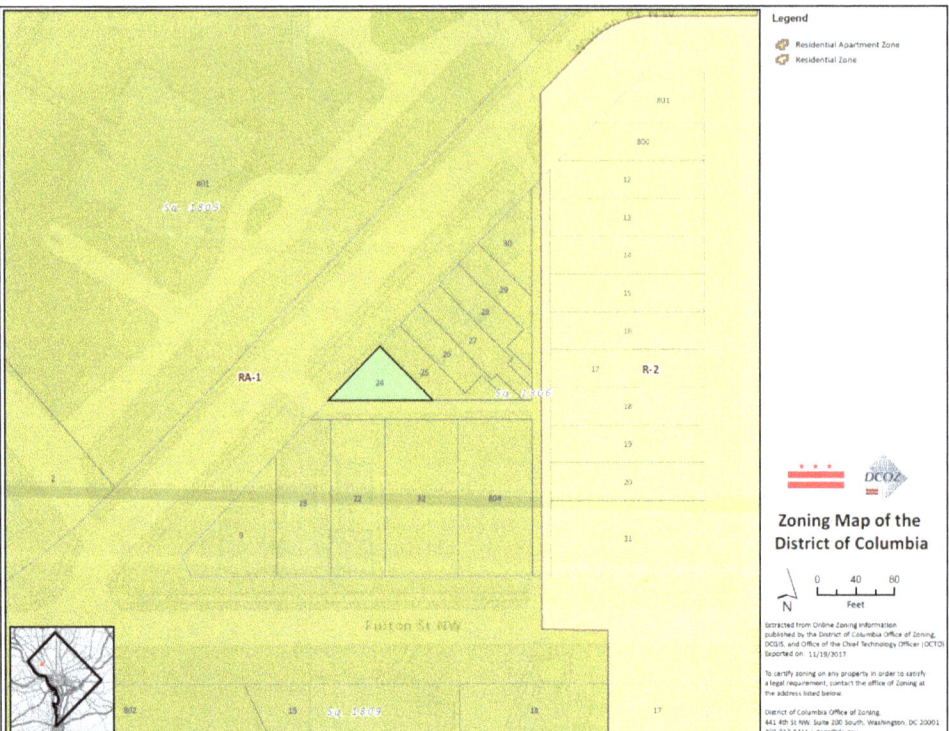

Figure 39 The Seven Townhouses – Looking Southwest

The view from the back of the townhouses (Figure 40) shows the staggered depth of the houses.

Figure 40 Rear View of the Townhouses

On March 6, 1968, Elkins secured a mortgage with the Columbia Federal Savings and Loan for the seven plots where the seven townhouses are today. The loan was for $343,000 and it is registered in Liber 12858, at folio 212, at the DC Register of Deeds.

The seven lots were posted as collateral with a trustee, The National Bank of Washington, as seven separate notes so that any one of the lots could be released when that specific note was paid in full. The notes ranged in value from $46,800 for lot 24 to $50,000 for lots 25 through 28.

By November 1968 Linde was advertising the townhouses as being under construction and open for inspection (**see** Error! Reference source not found.**41**).[107] The houses were all built on slabs thus there are no basements. The architecture is Federal style with different facades to include Mansard rooflines.

In 1977 *The Washington Post* ran a story on Linde, who at that point had worked in the DC Metropolitan Area for 18 years. He was a Harvard graduate who also did graduate work at the Wharton Business School. A 2002 story in *The Post* states he was granted his MBA and now lives in a house he built near the Washington National Cathedral.[108] While researching this book, I reached out to Linde at his home with a written note but did not receive a response.

Figure 41 Townhouse Advertisement November 1968

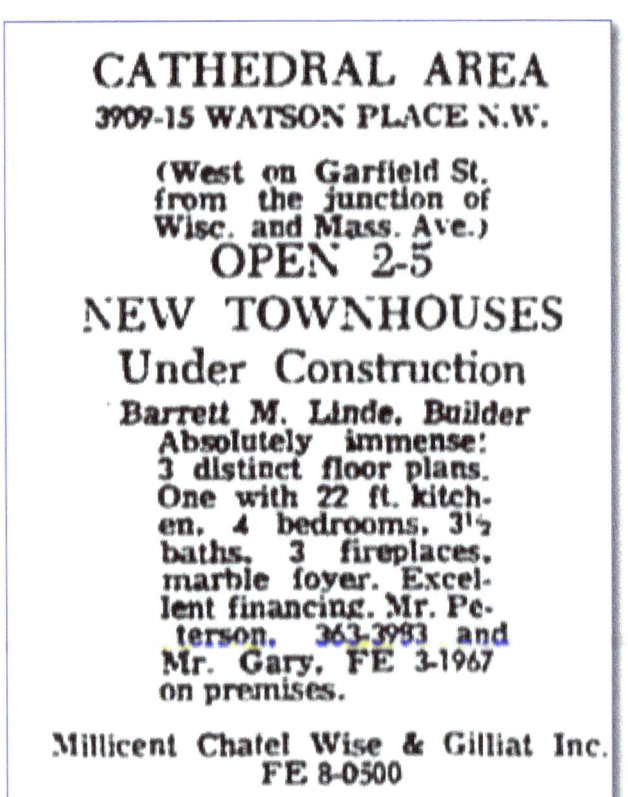

---

[107] *Sunday Star*, Nov. 3, 1968, page G-2
[108] Cavanaugh, Stephanie, "Barrett Linde, Still Ahead of Time," *The Washington Post*, March 30, 2002

A month later, in December, an advertisement (Figure 42) said there were just two townhouses left at $72,500 each. They were listed as a *truly extraordinary value in gracious in-town living for those needing large house features with minimum maintenance.* In addition to the features listed in the November advertisement, off-street parking was touted.[109]

Figure 42 Townhouse Advertisement December 1968

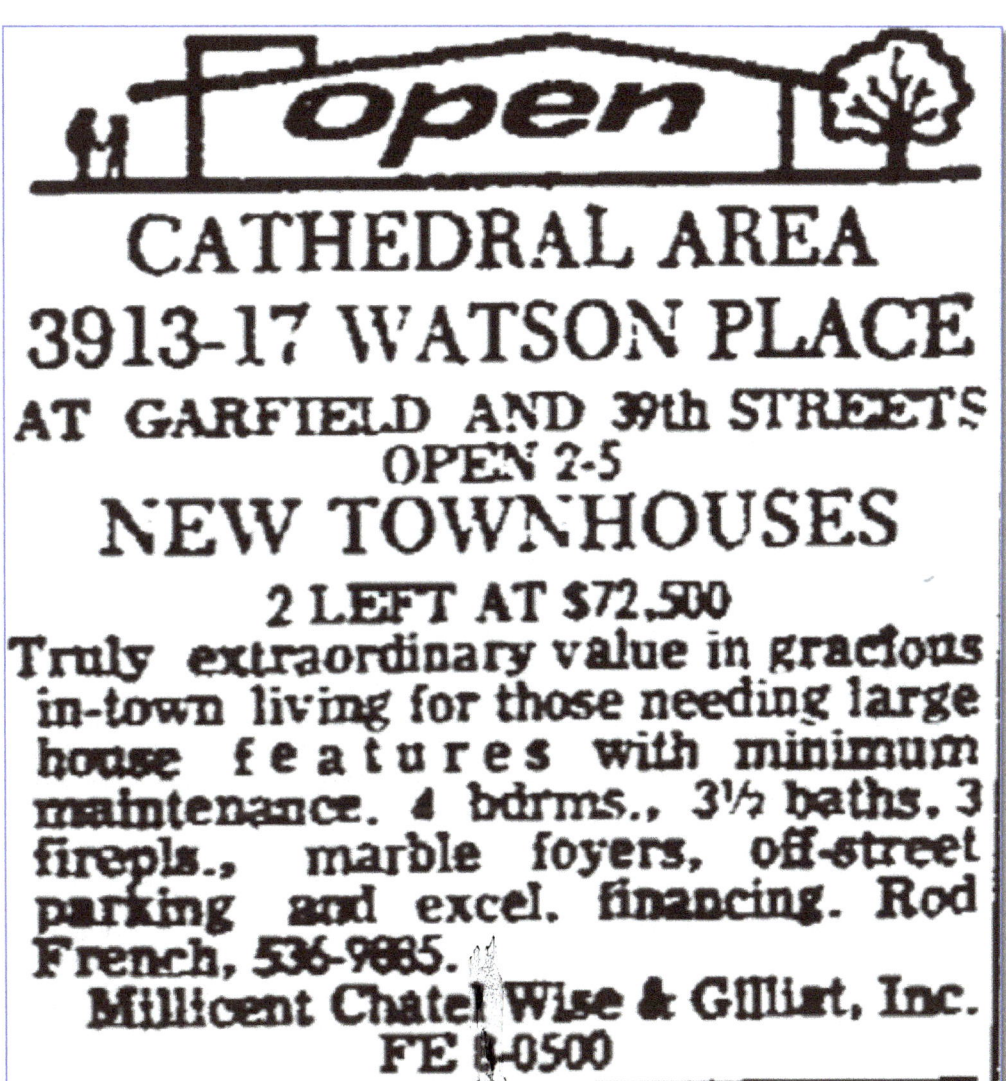

In mid-December 1968 John W. Truver sold one of the seven townhouses, 3915 Watson Place NW, to Llewellyn E. Thompson and his wife, Jane Thompson - Lot 27. The sale was recorded in Liber 12962 on folio 022, 29 January 1969.

The far right house of the seven, numbered 3921 Watson Place NW has four bedrooms, three full baths, and one powder room on three levels. This specific house

---

[109] *Evening Star*, Dec. 8, 1968, page 93 of the digital edition

was offered for rent, at $5,200 per month, on Coldwell Banker's website in September 2017. The web site picture is shown below as Figure 43.

The home is described as having a center entrance and there are bathrooms over the entrance – on both the second and third floors. The main floor has a marble foyer, a living room, kitchen, and a dining room as well as a powder room. Each of the upper floors has two bedrooms and two baths. There are three wood burning-fireplaces.

The advertisement sums up the attributes nicely:

> *Beautiful Federal style end-unit 4 bed 31/2 bath brick townhouse, NEW KITCHEN AND BATHS, features high ceilings and sunlight flooding the interior, gracious entrance with marble foyer, large rooms and 3 wood burning fireplaces. 2 kitchens and separate laundry. Convenient and charming LOCATION, walkable to Wisconsin/Mass Avenues, Cleveland Park, Glover Park, Georgetown & Glover Archibald Park!*

Figure 43 3921 Watson Place NW – From Coldwell Banker Advertisement

In Conclusion

With Ginger Elkins purchasing the land on the south side of Watson Place NW the transformation of the farm lands of the 27.5-acre parcel of Alliance Farm, Lucky Discovery, and Scott's Ordinary was nearing completion. Even when all of the housing was built – there were about 1,000 dwelling units – there was still much open space.

Just a year earlier, in 1966, George Scharffenberger joined City Investing Company when it was primarily a real estate holding company.

> *As chairman and chief executive of City Investing, he bought companies in the insurance, manufacturing, printing, housing, motel and food service industries. Well-known companies that City Investing owned wholly or in part included the Motel 6 chain, Rheem Manufacturing and the Sambo's restaurant chain.*

> *By the mid-1980's, diffuse conglomerates were out of fashion as corporate raiders took them over and broke them up for the greater value of their parts. Scharffenberger decided to take that route voluntarily. Among other sales, City Investing spun off Rheem and two other companies to Kohlberg Kravis Roberts & Company and Merrill Lynch Capital Markets in 1984. Shareholders ultimately received stock in the last remaining chunk, the Home Insurance Company. The liquidation produced $8 billion in value for shareholders, company officials said.*[110]

As part of the acquisition process, Scharffenberger approached my father quite a few times and directed him to sell a large real estate holding each time, as acquisitions were expensive. I recall my father saying that he foresaw the day when he might sell the last real estate holding and be out of a job. So he tendered his resignation and started his own real estate company in New Jersey, where our family lived. This was not too many years after Scharffenberger became CEO.

Thinking about the condominiums and cooperatives on the 27.5 acres as I finished this book I realized that each building has a glass door at its primary entrance. Then I recalled that Bob Dowling was the inventor of the glass door! This surprising fact is from the Nov. 5, 1960, edition of the *New Yorker Magazine* featuring a *Profiles* report on Dowling that runs from pages 61 through 113. Here is the relevant glass-door paragraph:

> *Dowling's career as an inventor dates back to 1935, when he was trying to think of a means of introducing light and a sense of spaciousness into the dark, cramped lobby of 40 Wall Street, a seventy-story building that the Starrett*

---

[110] George Scharffenberger obituary, *New York Times Business Day*, Dec 7, 2001

Corporation, which he was then working for, had erected five years before, Suddenly the idea of putting in glass doors came to him. "Everybody said it was impossible, and asked how I could lock such a door", *he recalls.* "I figured out a way of doing it by attaching metal strips at the bottom. We built a set of doors, using glass that was fired very hard, and installed them, and threw a big opening ceremony. Grover Whalen broke a bottle of champagne over one of the doors and didn't even scratch it, but I can tell you I was holding my breath. Then Hank Greenberg batted some baseballs as hard as he could against another one, and still nothing happened, so the doors were a great success."

Thus, 70 years after Dowling's City Investing bought the 27.5 acres, Dowling's presence can still be felt, not only in the mixed use of the land with its vast open spaces and the Victorian Gates but also in the little things like the glass doors and lobby walls.

Appendix I: A Brief History of City Investing Company

This description of City Investing is from the Lehman Brothers Collection – Contemporary Business Archives – Harvard Business School website.[111]

City Investing Company was founded by Robert E. Dowling in 1904 in New York City. It began as a small real estate office located at the corner of Columbus Avenue and 104th Street. In its first two years, City Investing bought $3.25 million in real estate in New York City, including the Coal and Iron Exchange Building in downtown Manhattan in January 1906. Later that year, City Investing began construction of a thirty-story office building in downtown New York that was described as the largest single building project ever undertaken by private capital in the city.

In the decades that followed, until the early 1950s, City Investing bought and sold properties and constructed new buildings and grew into one of the largest owners and managers of apartment and office buildings in New York.

In September 1953, the charter of City Investing was amended to broaden the types of businesses the company could engage in. It acquired Wilson Line, a company that operated excursion boats out of New York, Washington, and Boston in 1954.

In 1963 City Investing acquired an option to become a minority partner in a major real estate development in Calgary, Alberta. The site covered 100 acres owned by Canadian Pacific Railway Company.

The company acquired a majority interest in Supramar AG Switzerland, a leading company in hydrofoil boat design and development, in 1964. During the same year, City Investing also entered into a joint venture for the development of 3,300 acres in Texas City, Texas.

City Investing made a series of acquisitions that diversified the company considerably in 1967. In March it acquired all of the stock of Hayes International Corporation. In July it bought America Electric, Inc. In late 1967 it added Southern Financial Corporation and increased its stock ownership in General Development Corporation to 49 percent.

The company continued on its buying spree in 1968 by purchasing Rheem Manufacturing, ZD Products, Inc., Motel 6, Inc., and World Color Press, Inc., one of the

---

[111] https://www.library.hbs.edu/hc/lehman/company.html?company=city_investing_co

largest printers of magazines in the United States. In December 1968, it acquired a 96.78 percent interest in Home Insurance Company.

City Investing sold French & Company, an art-antiques dealer in New York, in 1969 and acquired a 51 percent interest in Guerdon Industries.

In 1970 a subsidiary of City Investing purchased the 82,000-acre San Cristobal Ranch, near Santa Fe, New Mexico, for $6.4 million. The company also added Westamerica Securities, Inc., during 1970 and continued to add to its portfolio of companies in 1971 by purchasing Acme Industries and Wood Brothers Homes. In 1972 it acquired United States Lumber.

By the early 1970s, City Investing had developed into a conglomerate with diverse holdings in housing, manufacturing, and real estate. The acquisitions helped boost sales from $150.7 million in 1967 to $542.0 million in 1971. Net income also rose dramatically during the same period, from $6.7 million to $57.3 million.

Appendix II: Robert W. Dowling's Biography

This biography is from the Dowling College, Oakdale, NY website[112]:

Robert Emmett Dowling died in 1943 and his son, Robert W. Dowling, took over the business. He retired from the company in 1972 after serving as president and, eventually, chairman of the board.

Dowling was instrumental in the planning and design of noteworthy residential New York City developments, such as Parkchester, Stuyvesant Town, and Peter Cooper Village. Dowling favored "tall, slender buildings on spacious grounds, with every apartment sunny and open, all done in good taste...." He applied this same aesthetic to other buildings as well, transforming numerous corporate and research institutions into pleasant, light-filled "campuses."

Dowling's real estate activities led to hands-on involvement in the arts. City Investing purchased and renovated several midtown theatres, and Dowling eventually became a producer for many notable Broadway shows and motion pictures. In 1950, he was appointed chairman for the fund-raising committee of the American National Theatre and Academy. As chairman of ANTA, Dowling visited Western Europe, Czechoslovakia, and Poland to "get acquainted with what European countries wanted in the way of United States entertainment...and what they had to export to these shores." In 1958, he traveled to Moscow and met with Soviet Premier Nikita Khrushchev to discuss "the exchange of United States and Soviet artists." In 1959, President Dwight Eisenhower tapped Dowling to head the Arts Advisory Committee of the National Cultural Center in Washington. Dowling proposed the design of the center, which later became the John F. Kennedy Center for the Performing Arts.

As a successful businessman, Dowling was a member of "64 civic, cultural, educational and professional organizations." Most significantly, he served as national president of the National Urban League (1950–1956), a group that advocated for equal economic opportunity for African Americans. He was a member of the National Conference of Christians and Jews and director of Boy Scouts of America. He chaired benefit committees for several organizations, including the Children's Village and Spence-Chapin Adoption Service. He served on the boards of many prominent businesses, such

---

[112] http://wwwx.dowling.edu/wikis/pmwiki.php/LISSHistory/BIOGRAPHYRobertWDowling

as the Waldorf-Astoria Corporation, R.H. Macy & Co., and Emigrant Savings Bank. He was also an early advocate for legalized off-track betting.

Dowling received a great deal of recognition for his civic and philanthropic work. In 1961, President John F. Kennedy cited Dowling as a man whose "dynamic dedication to all that is healthy in man and society is an inspiration." Dowling also received an honorary degree from Adelphi University.

A friendship with Adelphi's dean, Dr. Allyn T. Robinson, eventually led to Dowling's interest in Adelphi's Oakdale campus. In 1968, Dowling provided Adelphi-Suffolk College with an endowment of over $3 million. The grant allowed the college to become an independent institution, which was renamed in Dowling's honor in September 1968.

Appendix III: The Copped Hall History

This history is from the Copped Hall website[113] and emails from Alan Cox to the author.

Recorded history at Copped Hall starts in the 12th century when there was already a substantial building on the site. At that time Copped Hall belonged to the Fitzaucher family who served the King as huntsmen.

In 1303 the Copped Hall Estate consisted of 180 acres – comprising parkland, arable land and meadowland. In 1337 Copped Hall came into the hands of Sir John Shardlow who conveyed it to the Abbots of Waltham in 1350 in exchange for other lands. The Abbots described Copped Hall as "a mansion of pleasure and privacy". They were granted leave by Edward III in 1374 to extend the park by a further 120 acres on the Epping side.

In 1537 the Abbot gave Copped Hall to Henry VIII in the vain hope of saving Waltham Abbey from being dissolved. This failed to appease Henry and the Abbey was dissolved in 1540. Henry VIII visited Copped Hall but never lived there. In 1548 his son Edward VI allowed the future Queen Mary to live at Copped Hall where she remained – to a large degree – a prisoner, as she was a Catholic. When Mary became Queen in 1533, Copped Hall was leased to Sir Thomas Cornwallis. In 1558 it was transferred to the Duchy of Lancaster.

In 1564 Queen Elizabeth granted Copped Hall to her close friend - Sir. Thomas Heneage. Almost immediately he started to rebuild the mansion – incorporating part of the old house in the southwest corner. The building was complete by 1568 when Queen Elizabeth came to stay.

Sir. Thomas Heneage occupied high office - including Vice-Chamberlain of the Royal Household. In 1594, after his wife's death, he married the Countess of Southampton. Shakespeare's 'A. Midsummer's Nights Dream' was almost certainly written for their wedding celebrations and was first performed at Copped Hall in the long gallery after the wedding ceremony in London.

Lionel Cranfield, 1st Earl of Middlesex, acquired Copped Hall from the daughter of Sir Thomas Heneage in 1623. Cranfield became the Lord High Treasurer of England but

---

[113] http://coppedhalltrust.org.uk/

was disgraced and lived in retirement at Copped Hall until his death in 1645. While at Copped Hall he filled the house with treasures and extensively cultivated the garden.

Sir Thomas Webster owned Copped Hall from 1701 to 1738 but spent most of his time at his main house in Sussex. It seems that Copped Hall became rather dilapidated during his ownership. The foundations started to give way in one part and a hurricane damaged other parts. In 1739 the estate was sold to Edward Conyers whose son, John, demolished the mansion in 1748.

Edward Conyers son, John, inherited the property and considered repairing it as it had become dilapidated. However, John Conyers moved in cultural circles and wanted to express the latest architectural ideas of the day, which were incompatable with living in the old house. Plans for a Palladian mansion were drawn up by his architect - John Sanderson. Assisting with these ideas were Sir Roger Newdigate and another architect – Thomas Prowse. Very grand proposals were produced comprising a main block with a vast dome, a portico and attached curved colonnades leading to symmetrical pavilions. In the end only the main block was built - on a different site to the Elizabethan mansion. It was completed by 1758. Fragments of the Elizabethan house were retained and a rock garden was created in part of the cellars.

During the first part of the 19th century Copped Hall was little altered, its occupant, Henry Conyers (1782-1853) being more concerned with enjoying the place than improvements. His daughters did not appear to carry out any improvements before the estate was sold to George Wythes in 1869. George Wythes (1811-1883) was an extremely wealthy man who had made his fortune in the construction of railways and as a developer. George Wythes never lived at Copped Hall, but bought the estate for his only son George (1839-1875) who lived there until his early death. During this time the mansion was given a new wing to the north to accommodate the rapidly expanding sophistication of the service requirements of a large house.

After George Wythes junior died, his two young sons went to live with their grandfather at Bickley Park near Bromley and Copped Hall was let for a period to a Mr. Burns. In 1887, four years after their grandfather had died, the elder of these two sons (George Wythes 1867-1887) also died aged 19 - so when the younger son (Ernest Wythes (1868-1949) inherited he came into two fortunes - his own and his older brother's.

Ernest Wythes started spending immediately. In 1890 he commissioned one of the largest yachts in the Royal Yacht Squadron in which he sailed round the world. In 1894 he married a member of the aristocracy - Aline Thorold (1869-1951). His half-sister married the 4th Marquess of Bristol. Copped Hall simply was not grand enough and from 1893 Ernest Wythes set about making substantial improvements.

The stables were largely rebuilt and completed in 1894. In 1895 the fairly new wing was replaced by a larger one. The mansion roof line was given a balustrade and elaborate chimney tops. The stone architraves that existed on the east front were repeated on all the windows and the central portion of the west front was encased in stone featuring pillasters and carved pediment. The mansion forecourt was given grand railing screens with ornamental gates and piers. To the south a large elaborate stone conservatory or winter garden was built - with a glazed corridor linking it to the mansion. The inside of the house was extensively remodelled and filled with a very important collection of pictures, furniture and objects.

At the same time as the works to the mansion, an extensive Italianate architectural garden was constructed to the west of the mansion with temples, grand flights of steps, a parterre, gates, fountains and statuary. Other works were carried out in the gardens and on the estate.

By 1900 there were at least 31 gardeners and 27 house servants looking after the Copped Hall - together with all the farm workers. The Wythes were only at Copped Hall for part of the year. The rest of the time they were either at their house in London, in Scotland or abroad. When the family was not in residence the servants would clean the house and workmen would carry out building works.

The first world war changed life at Copped Hall. Many servants went off to the war – and did not come back. The land girls helped in the gardens and wounded soldiers were looked after by the family – especially by Ernest Wythes' three daughters. The family used to watch the zeppelins over London from the roof of Copped Hall.

During the war, in 1917, the main eighteenth century block of Copped Hall was largely burnt-out in a disasterous fire one Sunday morning. Much of the contents were saved but many items were also lost. The family moved to Wood House on the estate, which had been built by Ernest Wythes towards the end of the 19th century. The move was supposed to be temporary but in the end Mr. Wythes never rebuilt Copped Hall.

The gardens were all kept up until the second world war. The wing and the conservatory were untouched by the fire. The laundry and the stables and motor house were kept in use with their staff. The walled garden continued to produce flowers, fruit and vegetables – some of which were sold to Covent Garden. This produce supplied the Wood House and the London house.

Mr. Wythes died in 1949 and his wife died in 1951. The estate was sold in 1952 and at that time anything of value that could be stripped from the house and gardens was sold. The wing was stripped of its timberwork, the staircases were removed from the mansion and wing.

Railings and gates were sold, garden balustrading, statues, steps, etc. were mostly removed. Even many of the ancient specimen trees were cut down for their timber. The conservatory was eventually dynamited. Later the M25 was driven through a corner of the landscaped park.

Although this destruction was very serious, the essential identity of Copped Hall remained. The mansion shell was in surprisingly good condition - although it needed stabilising – and the structure of the gardens was still present. The motorway was at a sufficient distance from the house to be largely ignored. Copped Hall and its park was still a very attractive and historic place.

Copped Hall and its gardens lay derelict, abandoned and full of vandals for many years. From 1986 to 1992 there were a series of massive development proposals for the mansion, which were fought off by local people and architect - Alan Cox.

A charitable trust was set up in 1993 by Alan Cox and three local people to try and purchase the freehold of Copped Hall in order to restore it for educational, cultural and community purposes. This charitable trust had no money but were able to purchase the site in 1995 as a result of two low interest loans. It took five years to repay these loans. Since that time what Copped Hall has gone from strength to strength with much restoration carried out and our educational, cultural and community events well attended. The Copped Hall Trust benefits from substantial community support in the form of volunteers and donations. It is a much loved building and people regard it as a miracle that it has been saved.

The following picture of Copped Hall today (Figure 44) is from the Copped Hall Trust website.

Figure 44 Copped Hall Photograph with Morning Fog

Acknowledgments

In researching this book, Kathy's and my son, KC Higgins, an avid researcher, author of house histories, and coauthor of a book on Cleveland Park, was extremely helpful. It was KC who challenged me on the 1952 newspaper story on the so-called Georgian Gates at the Cathedral Avenue entrance to the Westchester campus. As a result of KC's urging I came into contact with the Copped Hall Trust and Alan Cox – a rich source of accurate information that lead to a delightful and open exchange of information.

Without the editing services of my good friend, Victoria (Vicki) Lemley, the book would be unfinished and reflect more of my enthusiasm for the subject than a polished product. One should never underestimate the value of a clear, independent review and Vicki has done that several times as I brought the work to a conclusion.

I have found the resources of both the District of Columbia Library's Special Collections (to include its online newspaper archives) and the District Recorder of Deeds online records to be critical in many research tasks.

The DC Library's Georgetown Branch's Peabody Room, so well managed by Jerry McCoy, has always been an important stop in any history research of the Georgetown area to include up the (now) Wisconsin Avenue corridor.

The research of Carlton Fletcher has proved to be invaluable. Fletcher is the researcher and writer at www.gloverparkhistory.com. His history online led me to other sources where I was able to get multiple perspectives on historical events. He has put a wonderful collection of old maps online, and I have used one of them as Figure 5 in this book.

Best Addresses, by James M. Goode, the 1988 edition, was another great source of information.

There are several websites that were helpful in finding historical facts and leads to other sources, among them:

- https://gov.kofiletech.us/DC-Washington/
- https://www.dclibrary.org
- http://gloverparkhistory.com/
- http://ghostsofdc.org
- http://coppedhalltrust.org.uk/

www.ingramcontent.com/pod-product-compliance
Lightning Source LLC
Chambersburg PA
CBHW080348170426
43194CB00014B/2727